W9-ANM-360

GRAMMAR AND BEYOND

Teacher Support Resource Book
with CD-ROM

Paul Carne

Jenni Currie Santamaria

Lisa Varandani

1

CAMBRIDGE
UNIVERSITY PRESS

CAMBRIDGE UNIVERSITY PRESS
Cambridge, New York, Melbourne, Madrid, Cape Town,
Singapore, São Paulo, Delhi, Tokyo, Mexico City

Cambridge University Press
32 Avenue of the Americas, New York, NY 10013-2473, USA

www.cambridge.org
Information on this title: www.cambridge.org/9781107694316

© Cambridge University Press 2012

This publication is in copyright. Subject to statutory exception
and to the provisions of relevant collective licensing agreements,
no reproduction of any part may take place without the written
permission of Cambridge University Press.

First published 2012

Printed in the United States of America

A catalog record for this publication is available from the British Library.

ISBN 978-0-521-14293-9 Student's Book 1
ISBN 978-0-521-14304-2 Student's Book 1A
ISBN 978-0-521-14307-3 Student's Book 1B
ISBN 978-0-521-27988-8 Workbook 1
ISBN 978-0-521-27989-5 Workbook 1A
ISBN 978-0-521-27990-1 Workbook 1B
ISBN 978-1-107-69431-6 Teacher Support Resource 1
ISBN 978-0-521-14330-1 Class Audio 1
ISBN 978-1-139-06183-4 Writing Skills Interactive 1

Cambridge University Press has no responsibility for the persistence or
accuracy of URLs for external or third-party Internet Web sites referred to in
this publication and does not guarantee that any content on such Web sites is,
or will remain, accurate or appropriate. Information regarding prices, travel
timetables, and other factual information given in this work is correct at
the time of first printing, but Cambridge University Press does not guarantee
the accuracy of such information thereafter.

It is normally necessary for written permission for copying to
be obtained in advance from a publisher. The tests on the CD-ROM
at the back of this book are designed to be copied and distributed in
class. The normal requirements are waived here and it is not necessary
to write to Cambridge University Press for permission for an individual
teacher to make copies for use within his or her own classroom. Only
those pages that carry the wording '© Cambridge University Press'
may be copied.

Layout services: TSI Graphics

Contents

Introduction

Grammar and Beyond is a four-level grammar series for beginning- to advanced-level students of North American English. The series focuses on the most commonly used grammar structures and their most common meanings and uses. It features a special emphasis on the application of these structures in academic writing. There is also a focus on authentic language use in communicative contexts.

A Unique Approach

Research Based

The grammar presented is strongly informed by the *Cambridge International Corpus*. This corpus was created from the research and analysis of over one billion words of authentic written and spoken language data gathered from college lectures, textbooks, academic essays, high school classrooms, and conversations between instructors and students. By using the *Cambridge International Corpus*, the series contributors were able to:

- Present grammar rules that reflect actual North American English
- Describe differences between the grammar of written and spoken English
- Focus more attention on the structures that are commonly used, and less on those that are rarely used, in both written and spoken language

Academic Writing Skills

The structure of *Grammar and Beyond* is designed to help students make the transition from simply understanding grammar structures to actually using them accurately in writing.

Error Avoidance

Each Student's Book unit features an *Avoid Common Mistakes* section that develops awareness of the most common mistakes made by English language learners and provides practice in detecting and correcting these errors. The mistakes highlighted in this section are drawn from the *Cambridge Learner Corpus,* a database of over 135,000 essays written by nonnative speakers of English.

Vocabulary

Every unit in *Grammar and Beyond* includes words from the Academic Word List (AWL), a research-based list of words and word families that appear with high frequency in academic texts. These words are introduced in the opening text of the unit, recycled in the charts and exercises, and used to support the theme throughout the unit. The same vocabulary is reviewed and practiced in the corresponding unit of *Writing Skills Interactive*.

Instructional Resources

Teacher Support Resource Book with CD-ROM

In addition to an answer key and audio script for the Student's Book, this book contains general teaching suggestions for applying any of the structures taught in the Student's Book to all four major skill areas.

The CD-ROM in the back of this book includes:

PowerPoint Presentations

Thirty-three animated presentations offer unit-specific grammar lessons for classroom use. Their purpose is to provide engaging visual aids to help clarify complex grammatical concepts while encouraging a high level of student involvement.

Unit Tests

Each of the 33 ready-made unit tests consists of two parts. Part I tests the grammar points in the order presented in the unit. Part II offers a more challenging blend of the grammar. Each unit test is easy to score on a scale of 100 points by following the guidelines included in the answer key, also found on the CD-ROM. Each unit test is available in two formats: as a PDF (portable document format) and as a Microsoft Word document. The Word documents are provided for those instructors who wish to customize the tests.

Online Unit-by-Unit Teaching Suggestions

The Unit-by-Unit Teaching Suggestions (downloadable at www.cambridge.org/grammarandbeyond) include unit-specific suggestions for expansion as well as the following suggestions.

- **Tech It Up:** Tips for using technology to practice the target grammar.
- **Beware:** Troubleshooting ideas for common problems with the target grammar.
- **Register:** Suggestions for addressing formality and native language usage as it applies to the target grammar.
- **Always an Exception:** Notes about exceptions to rules.
- **Game Time:** Ideas for games and other group activities that provide further practice.

Student Book Ancillaries

The following resources enhance the learning experience.

Class Audio CD

The Class Audio CD provides all Student's Book listening material for in-class use.

Workbook

The Workbook provides additional practice of the grammar presented in the Student's Book. All exercises can be assigned for homework or can be completed in class.

Writing Skills Interactive

Writing Skills Interactive is an online interactive program that provides instruction and practice in key skills crucial for academic writing (writing effective topic sentences, avoiding sentence fragments, distinguishing between fact and opinion, etc.). The units of *Writing Skills Interactive* correspond to and build on Student's Book units through shared vocabulary and themes.

Program Highlights

- Each unit includes an animated presentation that provides interactive, dynamic instruction in the writing skill.
- Academic and content vocabulary introduced in the corresponding Student's Book unit are recycled and practiced through the use of additional theme-based contexts.
- The presentation in each *Writing Skills Interactive* unit is followed by focused practice with immediate feedback.
- The program allows students to work at their own pace and review instructional presentations as needed. It is ideal for individual learning and practice, although it can also be used successfully in the classroom or computer lab.

General Teaching Suggestions

This guide provides a variety of strategies to use with recurring unit sections and exercise types in the *Grammar and Beyond* Student's Book. For expansion activities, technology-related activities, and ideas developed for individual units, refer to the Unit-by-Unit Teaching Suggestions, downloadable free of charge at www.cambridge.org/grammarandbeyond.

Student Self-Assessment

Refer to the Unit-by-Unit Teaching Suggestions (downloadable at www.cambridge.org/grammarandbeyond) for the list of objectives for the unit. Write them on the board, and ask students to copy them. Then have students do a brief self-assessment on each objective by choosing from the three options:

Self-Assessment, Unit _____

Objective _____

☐ 1. I know a lot about this and can use it easily.

☐ 2. I know something about this but need more practice.

☐ 3. I don't know very much about this.

Revisit the statements when you have completed the unit so that students can assess their progress.

Pre-unit Assessment Strategies

Prior Knowledge of Target Grammar

Before you begin the unit, you will probably want to do a brief assessment of students' prior knowledge of the grammar point. A grammar pre-assessment helps you determine whether students understand the meaning of the structure, whether they can produce the form, and whether they are able to integrate it into their writing and spontaneous speech. Here are some ways to help you obtain this information quickly.

- To determine whether students understand the target language, write several sentences on the board using the structure (for example, *John has lived in Washington for 10 years.*). Ask questions to elicit information about the meaning of the sentences. (*Does John live in Washington now? Did John live in Washington five years ago?*)
- To determine whether students can describe and reproduce the form, ask them to identify, for example, the part of speech, verb forms, or auxiliaries of the target structure. (*What is the verb in this sentence? What tense is it? How do you form the present perfect?*) Write two or three fill-in-the-blank sentences on the board, and ask students to complete them with the target structure.

(*There _____ several earthquakes this year. The reporter _____ a lot of questions.*) Ask students to complete the sentences. Walk around and spot-check their answers to assess students' familiarity with the structure.

- If most of the students are able to do the sentence completion, check their ability to use the grammar in a less controlled activity by asking a question to elicit the target language. (*What has the weather been like lately?*) Have them respond in writing with one or two complete sentences. Collect their work so you can assess the class as a whole (and not just a few students). You can also use this information for pairing and grouping later. Note the grammar used in students' responses, but do not correct or begin teaching the structure explicitly at this point. Tell students that they will be learning the structure in the upcoming unit. You may want to save your notes and write the students' sentences on the board when you have completed the unit so they can identify their errors and see solid evidence of their progress.
- If many of your students are able to produce the structure correctly in response to your question eliciting the target language, you can move more quickly through the controlled practice in the unit and spend more time focusing on the more open-ended writing and speaking activities. Tell students that although they may be familiar with the structure, it is your objective to help them put the grammar to use in their speaking and writing.

General Strategies for Unit Sections

Grammar in the Real World

This section introduces the target structure(s) in an authentic context, such as a website or short article. A *Notice* activity draws students' attention to the form or function of the target structures in the text. The following strategies can be used with this section. See the Unit-by-Unit Teaching Suggestions, downloadable free of charge at www.cambridge.org/grammarandbeyond.com, for text-specific notes and vocabulary lists.

Pre-reading/Warm Up

- Direct students' attention to the picture. Ask them to describe it, or ask specific questions about it (*What's happening? Who/Where do you think the person is?*). Ask students about their personal experiences or opinions related to the picture. (*Have you ever done this? How do you feel when this happens to you? What do you think about this?*)
- Ask students to read the title of the text and make one or two predictions about the content. Write students' predictions on the board. After they have read the text, compare their predictions to what they have read.

Pre-teaching the Vocabulary

Before students read, look through the text and make a list of words they may not know. Alternatively, use the word list, with Academic Word List (AWL) vocabulary labeled, found in the Unit-by-Unit Teaching Suggestions, downloadable free of charge at www.cambridge.org/grammarandbeyond. Try one or both of these techniques:

- List the words on the board, and ask students to discuss their meanings in small groups. Ask students for definitions. Make a note of words that students find difficult.
- List the words on one side of the board and their corresponding definitions on the other side (in a different order), and ask students to match them. Have students write down any words that are new. To save time in class, write the words and definitions on separate cards in advance and post them where students can see them.

Glossed Vocabulary

Paying attention to text signals, like footnotes, is an important academic skill. Therefore, you may not want to include the glossed vocabulary among the words you pre-teach. Instead, draw students' attention to the footnote numbers, and encourage them to watch for them while reading. Provide any clarification students need about the glossed words.

Comprehension Check

- To accommodate a variety of levels, have students complete the *Comprehension Check* individually. Write an additional comprehension question or a related question on the board for early finishers to answer.
- If you think the activity is too challenging for some of your students, have them compare their answers with a partner before you review the answers as a class. This gives students a low-stress way of checking their work. Consider pairing students of different levels based on your pre-assessment.

Notice

- The *Notice* activity guides students to find the target language in the text. Explain that scanning quickly for specific words is often an effective way to find the target language (for example, suggest that they look for the words *have* or *has* in a unit on the present perfect). To get them started, have students look at item 1 and tell you which word they should scan for.
- In some cases, you may want students to try to give answers before they look for them in the text. Ask students to share their answers. Then have students scan the article to find the correct answers.
- Have students do the first part of the activity (finding the target language) individually. Then have them work in pairs to discuss the question or complete the final part of the activity.

Grammar Presentations

Each unit includes at least one of these sections, which provide chart-based presentations of the target grammar. They address both structure and usage, and offer examples that reflect the unit theme. The section may also include a *Data from the Real World* box, providing real-world usage notes based on extensive corpus research.

Overview Box

Read the information in the overview box that introduces each set of grammar charts. Explain that this box highlights a key feature of the grammar point. Ask students what the connection is between the introductory information and the example sentences.

Grammar Charts

Teach students the value of the charts as a reference tool. When they make mistakes, ask them to look at the relevant chart to self-correct. If possible, keep a copy of the current chart(s) visible in the classroom for easy reference. Following are some ways to present the charts in class.

Structure Charts

Some charts, like the one that follows, break down the structure of the target language, with target language in bold. Here are some possibilities for teaching structure charts.

Time Context	Wh-Word	Would	Subject	Base Form of Verb	
In the past,	**how** **where**	**would**	I you he/she/it we they	**heat**	the water?

- Have students start the lesson with books closed. Write one of the examples from the chart on the board. Ask questions to check students' understanding of the grammar. (*What's the subject? What's the verb?*) Write labels above the example so that you are recreating the chart headings on the board. Ask students to provide additional examples to fit the pattern. Then have students open their books to study the chart.
- Have students repeat chorally, or call on individuals to read the questions/sentences in the chart.
- Use the chart to conduct a substitution drill. Call on individuals to say the sentences using, for example, a different verb.
- Use the chart for structured question-and-answer practice; that is, have one student ask a question using the words in the chart and another student give an appropriate answer.
- Have students write additional examples for the chart.

Usage Charts

Some charts, like the one that follows, contain usage notes on the left and example sentences on the right, with the target language in bold. Here are some possibilities for teaching usage charts.

a. Use subject pronouns to replace nouns in the subject position.	**Alison** wants to be more fit. **She** is taking an exercise class.
b. Use object pronouns to replace nouns in the object position.	Sara loves **exercise classes.** She takes **them** three times a week.

- Discuss each usage note and read the example sentences. Ask students to identify texts or conversations where they encounter the target language. For example, the imperative is often found in recipes and instructions. Elicit the target grammar by asking students questions. To check imperative forms, for example, you may ask, *Can anyone tell me how to make coffee?*
- Write a variety of examples on the board for each usage note (or distribute the examples on paper to students). Ask students to work in pairs to match the usage notes from the chart with the new examples.
- Ask students to work in small groups to come up with an additional example for each note. You can add challenge by asking students to incorporate the unit theme and any target vocabulary.

Additional Presentation Strategies

Photos and Art

Use pictures from magazines or the Internet. Talk about a picture using the target language. (*I think that before they got in the car, they had dinner at a nice restaurant. Now they're going to drive to the beach. They **have driven** down this road many times.*) Use a different picture to elicit the target language from students. (*What happened before this picture? What's going to happen next? What have they already done?*)

Time lines

Use time lines to talk about tenses. List events on the time line and ask questions to elicit the target grammar. (*What can you tell me about this person? How long has Maria had her job?*)

Unit-by-Unit Teaching Suggestions

Refer to the Teaching Suggestions for each unit for help with potential trouble spots with the specific target grammar, exceptions to the rules, and unit-specific chart presentation activities.

Grammar Application

This section follows each *Grammar Presentation* and gives students practice with the target grammar in a variety of contexts. The exercises progress from more controlled to more open-ended practice and incorporate the use of all four major skills (reading, writing, listening, speaking). Opportunities for personalization are also offered. A *Data from the Real World* box may be included as well, providing students with an opportunity to practice common real-life uses of the grammar point, giving them tools to make their English sound more natural.

This section of the Student's Book practices the target grammar in a variety of theme-related contexts. The recurring exercise types are listed below with classroom strategies given for each. See the Unit-by-Unit Teaching Suggestions for specific writing, speaking, and other expansion activities as well as suggestions for incorporating the use of technology.

Multiple Choice, Sentence Completion, and Matching Activities

For these activities, have students work individually. To ensure that students are processing the information and to expand on the activities, ask them to do one or more of the following:

- Explain the choice they made using information from the usage chart.
- Check and discuss their answers with a partner.
- Put another example on the board for their classmates to complete.

Listening Activities

Follow these steps with the listening activities.

1. Direct students to read the activity before they listen to help prepare them for what they will hear. To make the activity more challenging, have them guess the answers before listening.
2. Play the audio once all the way through at normal speed. Be sure to tell students that you will play it again. Then play it again, pausing after each item if students need time to finish writing. Play it a third time, again at normal speed.
3. When you reach the end of the exercise, direct students to read through it again. You may want students to compare their answers with a partner's so that they can check for potential errors.
4. Go over the answers by having students write them on the board (one student can write four or five answers), or project the exercise with an overhead or LCD projector, and complete it together.

Scramble Activities

Have students write the answers on the board. Tell them to be sure they haven't left out any words. They can do this by counting the number of words in the scramble activity and making sure it matches the number of words in their completed sentence.

Writing Activities

In these activities, students write or complete sentences with their own ideas. Be sure that they receive feedback on their work. Try one or more of these techniques:

- Have students share their sentences in small groups and then complete the activity on poster paper or on a regular piece of paper, choosing at least one sentence from each member. Post each group's paper so that other students can move around and see it. Tell students to find errors and correct them. Choose global errors to put on the board and discuss in depth with the entire class.
- Have students put sentences on the board. While they are writing, walk around and spot-check the work of other students.

Data from the Real World

These boxes contain research-based usage information, informed by the world's largest corpus. Go over them with the students. Where appropriate, ask for additional examples and discuss students' own impressions or "real world" experiences with the target language.

For example, if the box says, "You can use *someone* with imperatives: *Someone turn off the lights*," ask students where they might hear this sentence (*in a classroom, at work*). Ask students for additional examples.

The Unit-by-Unit Teaching Suggestions provide additional activities for practice of the information in these boxes.

Avoid Common Mistakes

This section presents a few of the most common learner errors associated with the target grammar, based on the world's largest error-coded learner corpus. It develops students' awareness of common mistakes and gives them an opportunity to practice identifying and correcting these errors in an editing exercise.

The information in this section is based on an extensive database of authentic student writing, so you can be sure that the errors indicated are truly high-frequency. This later gives students an editing focus. If you see these mistakes during unit activities (or even after you've moved on to later units), rather than correcting them yourself, refer students to the box in this section. The Unit-by-Unit Teaching Suggestions often provide further examples of common mistakes.

Editing Task

Have students work individually to complete the task and then compare answers with a partner. Do one of the following to correct the task.

- Once the task is complete, ask two or more students to read the corrected version aloud. Be sure to call on different students each time, so everyone feels accountable.
- Use an LCD or overhead projector to have students work together to correct it.
- Let students know if they miss a mistake, and tell them the category it falls under in the *Avoid Common Mistakes* box. Ask them to search the paragraph again.

Grammar for Writing

This section provides an assignment designed to support students as they learn to incorporate the target grammar in their own writing.

The Grammar for Writing box contains a quick review of the unit grammar as it relates to the writing assignment. Use the following strategies to teach each stage of this section.

Pre-writing Task

Follow these steps to complete the exercise:
1. Go over the information in the box, and tell students they will be focusing on these points for both the practice activity and the writing task.
2. Have students complete the practice activity individually and ask them to compare their answers with a partner.
3. Ask student for the answers. If possible, type the answers using a computer connected to an LCD projector, or write the answers on a copy of the page projected with an overhead projector.

Writing Task

Refer to the Unit-by-Unit Teaching Suggestions for unit-specific ideas and/or alternative writing tasks. Follow these steps for the activities in the book:
1. Help students come up with ideas in one of the following ways.
   - Ask questions to facilitate a whole-class brainstorming session. (*What does the writer of the* Practice *paragraph say about this topic? What are some things you might say about it?*)
   - Seat students in groups, and have each group brainstorm. Then have the groups share their ideas with the class.
2. Draw students' attention to features of the *Practice* paragraph, such as indentations, word choice, or use of the target grammar. Ask them to use the same features in their writing.
3. Assign the writing task as homework, or give students time to finish it in class. If you are doing the activity in class, set a time limit to help students stay on task.

Self- and Peer Editing

The following are strategies for encouraging both self- and peer editing.

- Have students read the editing tips in 2. *Self-Edit* and ask them to read through their writing and make changes as necessary.
- Have students exchange papers with a partner. Ask the partners to underline examples of the target language and check it against the *Avoid Common Mistakes* box. Have them circle any errors. Tell the partners to discuss any mistakes they found before they return the papers for revision.
- Have students peer-edit in groups of three, focusing on one paper at a time.
- Collect the students' writing and note the errors the students circle (or circle any mistakes with the target language that you see). Use these as examples in a follow-up lesson by writing the circled sentences on the board or typing them up and projecting them for class correction.

Grouping Strategies

It is difficult to overestimate the value of using a variety of grouping strategies in the classroom. In addition to making the class more dynamic, it helps you address different learning styles. Time for individual work is important because it allows students to process material in their own ways, but there are also many advantages to pair and group work.

Setting Up Groups

- **To create random groups,** pass out "four of a kind" items, such as colored slips of paper or playing cards. Then ask students to stand, and guide them to different areas of the room: *Everyone with a blue paper, come over here.* Alternatively, you can have students count off by threes or fours. Once they've counted, ask for a show of hands. (*All Number 1s, raise your hands.*) Then have all students with the same number sit together.
  Advantage: Helps build classroom community, challenges students to "get out of their shells," and increases the energy level of the class.
- **To create mixed-level groups,** use items that represent two or more levels. For example, pass out blue cards to higher-level students (or students who performed best on an assessment) and white cards to lower-level students. Tell students to form groups consisting of, for example, two blue cards and two white cards.
  Advantage: Allows for peer tutoring, gives lower-level students exposure to higher-level English, helps lower-level students feel like an integral part of the class.
- **To create same-level groups,** use the same strategy as for mixed-level groups (items to represent levels). Tell students to form groups of all white cards or all blue cards.
  Advantage: Allows you to tailor the activity to the level of the group (by simplifying it for the lower-level group or by making it more challenging/open-ended for the higher-level group).

Pair Work

- For pair work that involves collaborative work, you may want to pair students of similar levels so that one isn't doing all of the work. Or pair students of different levels and give each partner a distinct role. (*Partner A says the question, and Partner B writes it down.*)
- For pair-work activities that encourage repetition, like interviews and surveys, conduct a "walk-around." Have students walk around the room and ask questions to multiple classmates.

Strategies for Multi-level Classrooms

Every class has students at different levels, whether the class is designated "multi-level" or not. Following are some ways to help lower- and higher-level students within multi-level contexts. It is important to use a variety of strategies to address different student needs. Too much separation of lower-level students may make them feel as though they don't belong in the class, and too much peer tutoring may be frustrating for higher-level students.

Lower-level Students

Use one or more of these techniques for working with lower-level students:

- Adapt activities for lower-level students so that they can focus on one task. For example, provide a word bank so they only need to choose the word that belongs in a particular blank, or provide a sentence frame so they only need to supply, for example, the verb.
- Seat students in mixed-level groups and assign an easier role for lower-level students (for example, the reporter who reads the group's answers to the class).

Higher-level Students

- Provide more open-ended tasks for these students after they have completed the exercises in the book (for example, write sentences based on the grammar chart).
- Group higher-level students and give them a special project to complete while you work with lower-level students (for example, write a story using four words from the Academic Word List and at least two examples of the grammar point).

Class Audio Script

Unit 1

Exercise 3.2: Affirmative or Negative?
B (p. 10 / track 2)

1.

Carlos	Carlos Ramirez.
Kim	Hi, Carlos. It's Kim. How are you?
Carlos	I'm sick.
Kim	I'm sorry. Are you at home?
Carlos	No, I'm at work today. I'm so busy.

2.

Ana	Hi. This is Ana Cook. Sorry I'm not in my office. Please leave a message, and I will call you back.
Jane	Ana, this is Jane. Where are you today? Oh, right! I remember. It's Friday. You and your boss take a Spanish class on Friday. I'll call later.

3.

Juan	Juan speaking.
Barbara	Hello, Juan. This is Barbara. Are you at home?
Juan	Hi, Barbara. No, I'm not at home. I'm at the doctor's office with the children. I'll call you back later, OK?
Barbara	OK. Talk to you soon.

4.

Karen	Hello.
Karen's Mom	Hi, Karen, it's Mom. You're not in class today?
Karen	No, I'm with my classmates and my teacher. We're at the baseball game, at the stadium. I'll call you later.

5.

David	Hello. David Marks.
Friend	Hi, Dave. Where are you? At the stadium?
David	Well, no. I'm at home, the game's on TV.

6.

Drew	Hi! It's Drew at 732-555-6258. Leave me a message!
John	Hi, Drew! It's John. Ling and I are at the movie theater on Green Street. Come join us! Give me a call.

Unit 2

Grammar in the Real World
A (p. 14 / track 3)

Conversation A (Monday)

Yuko	So, is your next class writing?
Juan	No, it's reading.
Yuko	Really? My next class is reading, too. Are you in my class? It's at 1:30.
Juan	Maybe. Is your class in Building H?
Yuko	Yes, it's in Building H, room 308.
Juan	Then I'm in your class, too!
Yuko	Hmm. Where's Building H?
Juan	It's on the hill, over there.
Yuko	Oh, OK. What time is it?
Juan	It's 1:20. Uh-oh. We're late!
Yuko	No, we aren't.
Juan	Are you sure?
Yuko	Yes. Class is at 1:30.
Juan	Oh, you're right. That's good. Let's go.

Conversation B (Thursday)

Yuko	Hey, Juan. How are you?
Juan	I'm OK. How are you?
Yuko	I'm fine, thanks.
Juan	How are your classes?
Yuko	They're fine, but they're all really big.
Juan	Really? How many students are in your classes?
Yuko	About 25 to 30. Is that unusual?
Juan	No, it isn't. Who's your grammar teacher?
Yuko	Mr. Walters. He's funny, but his class is difficult.
Juan	So, when's your next class?
Yuko	Let me see. Today's Thursday. Computer lab is at 3:00.
Juan	When is it over?
Yuko	At 4:15. Let's meet after that.

Unit 3

Exercise 2.3: Pronunciation Focus: Plural Nouns
(p. 29 / track 4)

For nouns that end in the sounds /s/, /ʃ/, /tʃ/, /dʒ/, /ks/, and /z/, say /əz/ in the plural. These nouns have an extra syllable in the plural form.	**/əz/** /s/ class – classes /ʃ/ dish – dishes /tʃ/ watch – watches /dʒ/ message – messages /ks/ box – boxes /z/ quiz – quizzes
For most other nouns, say /s/ or /z/ in the plural.	**/s/ or /z/** boo**k** – books pho**ne** – phones accessor**y** – accessories

A (p. 30 / track 5)

1. purse; purses
2. bag; bags
3. map; maps
4. door; doors
5. size; sizes
6. computer; computers
7. page; pages
8. closet; closets
9. phone; phones

Unit 4

Exercise 2.3: Demonstratives Without Nouns
B (p. 43 / track 6)

Jane	How much are these?
Salesclerk	$30.
Jane	Thank you. That's a nice computer.
Lisa	Yes, it has a big screen. What's that on the front?
Salesclerk	It's the webcam. And here's the headphone jack.
Jane	Yeah. Is this a new model?
Salesclerk	No. This is an old model. That's why it's on sale. That's the new model over there.
Jane	Oh, I see. Hey, these are great headphones.
Lisa	Yeah? Buy them!
Jane	Hmmm . . . They're $250. No, thank you!

Unit 5

Exercise 3.1: Questions with *What . . . like?*
B (p. 58 / track 7)

John	I have exciting news! I have a new job!
Erica	That's great!
John	Well, the bad news is this: It's in St. Louis. It's not here in Chicago.
Erica	Wow! What's St. Louis like?
John	It's an old Midwestern city in Missouri.
Erica	What's the weather like in the winter?
John	It's very cold, and it's snowy.
Erica	What are the people like?
John	They're very friendly.
Erica	What are the restaurants like?
John	They're good and not too expensive.

Unit 6

Exercise 2.2: Prepositions of Place: Things in the Neighborhood
B (p. 67 / track 8)

1.

Woman 1	Where are you?
Man 1	I'm in the parking lot.
Woman 1	Where's that?
Man 1	It's in front of the supermarket.

2.

Man 2	Are you at the bookstore?
Woman 2	No. I'm at the hair salon.
Man 2	Where's that?
Woman 2	It's above the coffee shop.

3.

Man 3	Where are you and Steve?
Man 4	We're inside the movie theater.
Man 3	Where's the movie theater?
Man 4	It's across from the supermarket.

4.

Woman 3	Where are you?
Woman 4	I'm at the park with my dog.
Woman 3	Where's the park?
Woman 4	Next to the school.

5.

Man 5	Where's the post office?
Woman 5	It's across from the school.
Man 5	OK. Thanks.

Unit 7

Exercise 2.3: *There Is / There Are* or *It Is / They Are*
B (pp. 81–82 / track 9)

Hi, my name is Mi-Sun. My hometown is Concord, Massachusetts. It's a small historic town near Boston.

There are some historic buildings in Concord. They're very old. There are also a lot of small shops. They're usually expensive.

There's an old hotel. It's called the Colonial Inn. It's a popular place for lunch and dinner. There are a lot of special events at the hotel, like weddings and meetings. There's often live music at night. I like to go and listen to jazz.

There's a national park by the Concord River. It's beautiful and peaceful. There are always lots of tourists at the park. It has a famous bridge – Old North Bridge. Also, there's a very famous statue of a minuteman next to the bridge. The soldier was called a "minuteman" because he could get ready in a minute. A historic battle happened there in 1775. I often walk there with friends.

Unit 8

Exercise 2.4: Pronunciation Focus: -s and -es
(p. 93 / track 10)

Say /s/ after /f/, /k/, /p/, and /t/ sounds.	*laughs, drinks, walks, sleeps, writes, gets*
Say /z/ after /b/, /d/, /g/, /v/, /m/, /n/, /l/, and /r/ sounds and all vowel sounds.	*grabs, rides, hugs, lives, comes, runs, smiles, hears, sees, plays, buys, goes, studies*
Say /əz/ after /tʃ/, /ʃ/, /s/, /ks/, /z/, and /dʒ/ sounds.	*teaches, pushes, kisses, fixes, uses, changes*
Pronounce the vowel sound in *does* and *says* differently from *do* and *say*.	do /duː/ → does /dʌz/ say /seɪ/ → says /sez/

A (p. 93 / track 11)

laughs
drinks
walks
sleeps
writes
gets
grabs

rides
hugs
lives
comes
runs
smiles
hears
sees
plays
buys
goes
studies
teaches
pushes
kisses
fixes
uses
changes
do; does
say; says

C (p. 94 / track 12)

1. Staci goes to school from Monday to Friday from 7:30 a.m. to 11:30 a.m.; goes
2. Then she rushes to work.; rushes
3. She works at a hospital until 8:00 p.m.; works
4. In the evening, Staci catches a bus to go home.; catches
5. On her way home, she listens to music and relaxes.; listens
6. On her way home, she listens to music and relaxes.; relaxes
7. She eats a quick dinner with her family.; eats
8. Then she reads to her children and checks their homework.; reads
9. Then she reads to her children and checks their homework.; checks
10. If she isn't too tired, she finishes her own homework.; finishes
11. Staci usually falls asleep by 10:00 p.m.; falls

Unit 9

Exercise 2.3: Pronunciation Focus: *Do you . . . ?*
(p. 106 / track 13)

In speaking, people often say *Do you* very fast. It can sound like one word ("D'you"). Always write *Do you* as two words, but say it fast so it sounds like one word ("D'you").

A (p. 106 / track 14)

Do you fall asleep with music on?
Do you like loud music?
Do you dance when you listen to music?
Do you listen to music all the time?
Do you study with music on?
Do you sing along to music?
Do you have an MP3 player?

Unit 10

Exercise 2.4: Pronunciation Focus: Intonation in Questions
(p. 116 / track 15)

In information questions, our voice usually *goes down*. We call this falling intonation.	Where do you go on va**ca**tion? Why do you stay **home**? When do you see your **re**latives?
In *Yes / No* questions, our voice often *goes up*. We call this rising intonation.	Do you celebrate Me**mor**ial Day? Is that your favorite day of the **year**? Does she work at **night**?

A (p. 116 / track 16)

1.
Man   Excuse me. Are you from Japan?
Woman   Yes, I am. I'm from Tokyo.
2.
Man   Can I ask you some questions?
Woman   Sure!
3.
Man   What's your favorite holiday in Japan?
Woman   New Year's Day.
4.
Man   Why is it your favorite?
Woman   Because we have special food for the holiday, and we relax all day.
5.
Man   Do you help your mother with the cooking?
Woman   Yes, I do. We also see all our relatives on New Year's Day.
6.
Man   Do you play any special games?
Woman   No, not really. But we watch some special TV programs.
7.
Man   What else do you do on New Year's Day?
Woman   Well, we read all our holiday cards then.
8.
Man   Do you really save all the cards to open on the same day?
Woman   Yes, it's a special custom.

B (p. 116 / track 17)

Are you from Japan?
Can I ask you some questions?
What's your favorite holiday in Japan?
Why is it your favorite?
Do you help your mother with the cooking?
Do you play any special games?
What else do you do on New Year's Day?
Do you really save all the cards to open on the same day?

Unit 11

Exercise 3.2: The Position of *Because*
(p. 128 / track 18)

1. Leo works at night because he goes to school during the day.
2. Tony can only study in the mornings because he thinks more clearly then.
3. Because Bob's alarm clock doesn't work, he is always late.
4. Jamal can't study at home because his roommates are too noisy.
5. Because Leo forgets to write his assignments down, he often misses them.
6. Tony and Jamal sometimes miss class because they play basketball instead.

Unit 12

Exercise 2.3: Pronunciation Focus: Saying Simple Past Verbs
(p. 139 / track 19)

When the verb ends in /t/ or /d/, say -*ed* as an extra syllable /ɪd/ or /əd/.	**/ɪd/ or /əd/** /t/ wai**t** → waited /d/ deci**de** → decided
When the verb ends in /f/, /k/, /p/, /s/, /ʃ/, and /tʃ/, say -*ed* as /t/.	**/t/** /f/ lau**gh** → laughed /k/ loo**k** → looked /p/ sto**p** → stopped /s/ mi**ss** → missed /ʃ/ fini**sh** → finished /tʃ/ wat**ch** → watched
For verbs that end in other consonant and vowel sounds, say -*ed* as /d/.	**/d/** liste**n** → listened cha**nge** → changed li**ve** → lived pl**ay** → played ag**ree** → agreed borr**ow** → borrowed

A (p. 139 / track 20)

waited
decided
laughed
looked
stopped
missed
finished
watched
listened
changed
lived
played
agreed
borrowed

Exercise 3.2: Pronunciation Focus: Saying Irregular Simple Past Verbs
(p. 143 / track 21)

Sometimes the spelling of two verbs is the same, or similar, but the pronunciation is different.	read → read say → said BUT pay → paid hear → heard
Sometimes the letters *gh* are not pronounced.	buy → bought think → thought
When you learn an irregular verb, learn the pronunciation, too.	

A (p. 143 / track 22)

read; read
say; said
pay; paid
hear; heard
buy; bought
think; thought

Unit 13

Exercise 3.1: Simple Past Information Questions and Answers
B (p. 155 / track 23)

Today, we have some successful young business owners. We want to find out two things: Why were they successful? What can we learn from them?

The first person is Shelly Hwang – a good example of a successful small business owner. Well, she started out small, but now her business is quite big. Hwang is from South Korea. She moved to Los Angeles when she was 19-years-old to study business. After college, she started several businesses, but they were not successful. Then her business partner, Young Lee, had the idea of a frozen yogurt store. She and Lee developed the business concept together. Lee also designed the inside of the store – it was very modern and simple. The idea was to have simple, fresh, and healthy frozen yogurt. She opened her first Pinkberry store in California in 2006. The first store only had two flavors: original and green tea.

Customers liked Pinkberry because the yogurt wasn't too sweet. Pinkberry became very popular. Hwang expanded her business in 2008, and she now has a lot of stores across the United States.

Unit 14

Exercise 3.1: Simple Past of *Be: Yes / No* Questions
B (p. 164 / track 24)

Tanya	Grandpa, can I ask you some questions for my school assignment?
Grandfather	Of course. I hope I can answer them.
Tanya	Don't worry. They're easy questions. First of all, when were you born?

Grandfather	I was born in 1940.
Tanya	And were you born in New York City?
Grandfather	No, I wasn't. I was born in Turkey. I came here when I was two.
Tanya	Oh, I didn't know that. Now, was your family large?
Grandfather	Oh, yes. There were five girls and two boys.
Tanya	And your brother – my great-uncle Steve – was he a good student?
Grandfather	Ha, ha. No, he wasn't. But he's a very successful businessman now.
Tanya	Were you and your brother good friends?
Grandfather	Oh, yes. We were like best friends.
Tanya	And your sisters? Were they nice to you?
Grandfather	Do you want the truth? No, not really.
Tanya	That's sad. Were you and your sisters the same age?
Grandfather	No, we weren't. They didn't pay much attention to me or my brother because we were so little. But later, that changed.
Tanya	All of the children worked at your father's store. Was it near your house?
Grandfather	Yes, it was downstairs! We lived upstairs. I was never late for work!

Unit 15

Exercise 2.2: Ordering Events
A and C (pp. 174–175 / track 25)

About a year ago, my friend Leo was almost a scam victim. One morning, he saw an e-mail from his bank before he went to work. When he opened the e-mail, it said, "You have a new account number. Write your old account number here so we can check your identity." He didn't have time to reply before he left home. Before he left for work, he wrote a note to his wife, "Please reply to the bank's e-mail." Then he left for work.

When he got to the subway station, he bought a newspaper. After he got on the train, he met a co-worker and they talked. When he read the newspaper at lunchtime, he read an article about a bank Internet scam. He realized the e-mail from the bank was that scam. After he read the article, he called his wife. Luckily, when his wife read the e-mail, she realized it was a scam and deleted the e-mail.

Unit 16

Exercise 3.2: *How Much . . . ?* and *How Many . . . ?*
A (p. 189 / track 26)

Gina	OK. So what do we need for the picnic?
Tomo	Well, how many students are there in the class?
Gina	There are 18 students, plus the teacher, so that makes 19 people.
Tomo	How much money do we have?
Gina	We have $90.
Tomo	$90?

Gina	Right. That's $5 for each student. The teacher doesn't pay.
Tomo	Oh, right.
Gina	I have all the choices here, so . . . you write the list, OK?
Tomo	OK. How many people want water? How many bottles of water do we need? Um . . . 8, 9, 10. Ten for water.
Gina	Ten bottles of water. How much juice do we need? I guess nine bottles, right?
Tomo	Yeah. Nine bottles of juice.
Gina	Right. Now the food.
Tomo	OK, so how many people want sandwiches? Let's see . . . four, five, six. Six. And the rest want chicken salad.
Gina	OK. How many bags of potato chips?
Tomo	Uhh . . . 16 for potato chips.
Gina	What's next? Oh, salad and vegetables. How much salad do we need?
Tomo	Fourteen bowls of salad and 5 want vegetables.
Gina	Fourteen? OK. So now how much cheese and how many cookies?
Tomo	Ten people want cookies and nine want cheese and crackers, so what do you think? A pound of cheese?
Gina	Yeah. A pound of cheese is fine. So that just leaves the fruit.
Tomo	Yeah, so how many people want oranges?
Gina	Fifteen want an orange. So 15 oranges.
Tomo	And how much watermelon do we need?
Gina	Four pieces of watermelon.
Tomo	Great. That's it.

Unit 17

Exercise 3.2: *A Lot Of, A Little, A Few,* or *Many*
(pp. 202–203 / track 27)

Karina's English class at Dixon College is very international. Her class has a few Russians: Karina and two others. There are many students from Brazil, perhaps 80 percent. There are a few students from Japan, but not many. The rest are from other Asian countries like Malaysia, Thailand, and Vietnam.

They come from all over the world and bring interesting stories with them. Rosa is from São Paulo, Brazil, and listens to a lot of Brazilian music. She loves it. She also has a few songs from Puerto Rico on her computer, but not many. Seri, from Penang, has a lot of beautiful furniture from Malaysia in her house. Keiko, from Japan, taught Karina and Rosa a little Japanese, but the words are difficult to remember. Noom, from Bangkok, loves his country's food. Sometimes he makes a little Thai food for his classmates, but not much because it's very hot for them. Linh, who moved from Vietnam, eats a lot of spicy food. She loves it! Sometimes Karina brings in a little *borscht*, a Russian soup. Only Keiko and Noom like it, so she doesn't make a lot of it. The best part of Karina's diverse class is that she can hear many languages besides English every day!

Unit 18

Exercise 2.2: Pronunciation Focus: Pronouncing *A* and *An*
(p. 214 / track 28)

We pronounce *a* and *an* with a weak sound /ə/ or /ən/, because we don't stress the articles.	*a decision*	*an analyst*
	a business	*an ostrich*
	a risk	*an opinion*

A (p. 214 / track 29)

a decision
a business
a risk
an analyst
an ostrich
an opinion

Unit 19

Exercise 2.3: Possessive Pronouns, Possessive Determiners, and Verbs
A (p. 229 / track 30)

Sara   Kyla, let's cook dinner!

Kyla   Wow, your kitchen is complicated. Look at all the shelves!

Sara   Well, that's Franny's shelf. She eats a lot of junk food. Those bags of chips are hers. As you can see, her shelf is full of chips and candy.

Kyla   It looks like Su's shelf is full of healthy things.

Sara   Yes. Those vitamins are hers. Her shelf is always very neat, too. Su and Mari share one shelf. That top shelf is theirs. It always has baskets of fruit on it.

Kyla   Which shelf is yours?

Sara   This one is mine.

Kyla   Oh, so are those your bowls?

Sara   Yes, those are mine. They're from Japan.

Kyla   They're very pretty. Whose things are on this shelf?

Sara   Oh, those are ours. We all share that shelf. OK. Well, let's start cooking.

Kyla   Right. So, who's coming for dinner tonight?

Sara   Our families! We have a lot of cooking to do.

Unit 20

Exercise 2.5: Imperatives with *Always* and *Never*
A (p. 246 / track 31)

Female Announcer   This is a travel-guide podcast brought to you by the Radio Connections team. This week's podcast is about Brazil.

Male Announcer   Brazil is a wonderful place to visit, work, or study. But before you get there, there are some things you need to know about the social customs. We asked a team of young people who visited Brazil last year to write a list of *Dos* and *Don'ts* for us. Here's their podcast.

Female Student   Here's tip number 1: This is very important for tourists: When you speak with someone, always look them in the eye. Showing steady eye contact shows that you're engaged in what they're saying.

Most people in Brazil like to give their hostess extra time to finish getting ready. For this reason, they often come to parties late. Never arrive at parties early.

Male Student   Always bring your hostess a small gift. Flowers are common.

Female Student   The next tip is about eating. In Brazil, people don't carry a meal with them when they walk to class or work. It's generally not a good idea to eat food in class.

Male Student   In restaurants, waiters don't want you to feel rushed, so they won't bring your check until you ask for it. When you go to a restaurant and are ready to leave, always ask your server for the check.

Female Student   Finally, most people leave a 10 percent tip. So, if you don't leave a tip, you look very rude.

Male Announcer   Have a great trip and enjoy your stay in Brazil.

Female Announcer   This was a travel guide podcast brought to you by the Radio Connections team.

Unit 21

Exercise 2.2: Pronunciation Focus: Saying *Can* and *Can't*
(p. 255 / track 32)

Sometimes it's hard to hear the difference between *can* and *can't*.	
People usually do not pronounce the *a* in *can* very clearly.	*I can use a laptop* usually sounds like *I c'n use a laptop.* *Can I use your phone?* usually sounds like *C'n I use your phone?*
People always say the *a* in *can't* very clearly.	*I can't use an e-reader.* *He can't find his phone.*
In short answers, people always say the *a* in *can* and *can't* clearly.	*Yes, I can.* *No, I can't.*

A (p. 255 / track 33)

1. I can use a laptop.
2. I can't use a laptop.
3. I can design a blog.
4. I can't design a blog.
5. He can find his phone.
6. He can't find his phone.

B (p. 255 / track 34)

Ji-Sek	I joined Gen 5. I like it better than Linkage.
Carol	Really? Why?
Ji-Sek	Well, on Gen 5 you can chat with your friends. On Linkage, you can't chat.
Carol	That's true. But I don't really want to chat. On Linkage you can join interest groups. Can you do that on Gen 5?
Ji-Sek	Yes, you can. I joined two interest groups last night.
Carol	Well, on Linkage you can download songs. Can you do that on Gen 5?
Ji-Sek	Yes, you can. I downloaded a song this morning.
Carol	Can you send songs to your friends on Gen 5?
Ji-Sek	No, you can't send songs to friends on Gen 5. Can you do that on Linkage?
Carol	Yes. I like that about Linkage. You can send songs to anyone. It's very easy.
Ji-Sek	Oh. I didn't know that.
Carol	Yes. And on Linkage, you can find a job. That's important. Can you do that on Gen 5?
Ji-Sek	No, you can't find a job on Gen 5. But you can post pictures on it. Gen 5's good for that.
Carol	Oh. You can't post pictures on Linkage. It's not that kind of site.

Unit 22

Exercise 2.1: Using *Can*, *Could*, and *Would* in Requests and Answers

A (p. 268 / track 35)

Elena	I need to talk to Professor Baker. Can you tell me what building he's in?
Freda	Yeah, sure. He's in the Ross Building. I'm going there now. Come on! So, what's up?
Elena	Oh, it's just a problem about the exams. Can you come with me to Professor Baker's office? Do you know where it is?
Freda	Yeah, sure. I met with him last semester.
Elena	When I finish with the professor, can we meet up again later?
Freda	Yeah, good idea.
Elena	Just one problem. I don't know what time the meeting finishes. Can you wait for me in the cafeteria?
Freda	No problem. I can do my homework.
Elena	Hello, Professor Baker. Do you have a minute?
Prof. Baker	Certainly. Would you close the door, please?

Elena	Of course. Could you help me, please? I have an exam next Tuesday, and I have a family wedding on that day. Would you write a letter to the exam professor about this?
Prof. Baker	Oh, I'm sorry. I can't. A family wedding is not an excuse to miss an exam. That's the college's policy.
Elena	Oh! Really?
Prof. Baker	I'm very sorry. Those are the rules.
Elena	Oh, well, OK. Thank you for your time.

Unit 23

Exercise 2.4: Negative Contractions
(p. 284 / track 36)

Carla	Hey, Rod. You're not studying today?
Rod	No, Chris isn't coming to class today.
Carla	You're doing a project together, right?
Rod	Yes, with Jon, Lisa, and Cristina, but it isn't going well. We aren't getting along well, either.
Carla	Really? Why not?
Rod	Well, Chris isn't doing his share of the work. He isn't reading the books, and he isn't coming to meetings with the group.
Carla	What do the others in the group think?
Rod	They aren't feeling too happy with him. In fact, they aren't speaking to him. We wrote a letter to the teacher about him.
Carla	Maybe it's time to talk to him about it. I know he isn't doing a good job, but maybe there's a reason for it.
Rod	I guess we aren't giving him a chance to explain.

Unit 24

Exercise 3.1: Past Progressive and Simple Past
B (pp. 302–303 / track 37)

Accidental Discoveries!

Sometimes, unexpected things happen, and someone invents or discovers something. The discovery of gravity – the force that pulls all the stars and planets to each other in the universe – is an example of this. In 1666, Isaac Newton, an English scientist, was sitting in his garden when an apple fell from an apple tree. Newton got the idea of gravity from that one moment.

Another story is about James Watt, who was born in 1736. Some people say that while James Watt was looking at a boiling tea kettle, he got the idea for a steam engine.

In 1799, French soldiers were working in Egypt when they found a stone with writing on it. This was the famous Rosetta Stone. The stone helped people learn how to read Egyptian writing.

In 1908, while a German woman was making a cup of coffee, she discovered that paper worked as an excellent filter for coffee and water. She invented coffee filters.

In 1895, a German scientist was experimenting with electricity when he noticed that one piece of equipment was creating some strange green light around some objects. While he was working, he noticed that the stripes of light – or rays – went through paper but not thicker objects, and through humans but not through bones. By 1900, scientists everywhere were working with the new rays, and doctors were using X-rays to take pictures of people's bones.

It's amazing that all these inventions and discoveries happened by accident!

Unit 25

Exercise 3.1: Using *Who* and *What*
B (pp. 314–315 / track 38)

Ana Maria	Hi! My name is Ana Maria. What did you eat for lunch today?
Philip	I ate a garden salad.
Ana Maria	Who did you eat with?
Philip	I ate with my roommate here, Mike.
Ana Maria	Hi! What did you have for lunch?
Mike	I had a chicken sandwich and fresh tomato soup.
Ana Maria	Thanks! Excuse me, can I ask you some questions? Who usually cooks your dinner?
Maya	My mom usually does.
Ana Maria	What is your favorite dish?
Maya	It's definitely my mom's orange chicken. It's great.
Ana Maria	Thanks so much!

Unit 26

Exercise 2.2: Pronunciation Focus: Saying *To*: *Want To, Would Like To*
(p. 324 / track 39)

In natural speech, people say *to* quickly. It can sound like /ta/ or /tə/.	*Children like to play on computers.* *She wanted to share her pictures.*
Want to often sounds like "wanna."	CONVERSATION *What do you want to do?* *Do you want to go?*
Do not use "wanna" in writing and formal speaking.	FORMAL SPEAKING *In this presentation, I want to talk about three problems.*
People say *'d* softly in *I'd like to*.	*I'd like to join that new social networking site.*

A (p. 324 / track 40)

Children like to play on computers.
She wanted to share her pictures.
What do you want to do?
Do you want to go?
In this presentation, I want to talk about three problems.
I'd like to join that new social networking site.

B and C (pp. 324–325 / track 41)

Vic	What do you want to do as a career?
Bryan	I'd like to be a teacher. You know, I really want to teach elementary school. I like to work with children. How about you?
Vic	Well, I want to have my own business one day.
Bryan	Really? So, what kind of business do you hope to have?
Vic	Well, I'd like to work with computers somehow. Computers are my hobby right now. I actually like to spend time in front of a screen.
Bryan	So, how do you do that? I mean, what do you need to do?
Vic	I guess I need to stay in college another year and develop my computer skills.

Unit 27

Exercise 2.3: *Be Going To* or Present Progressive
A (p. 340 / track 42)

Welcome, students, and thank you for coming today! As you know, we're all here because of your efforts to help Redview Community College become a better place of learning! With your help, we now have enough money to begin improvements.

First, we're replacing all the old computers in the library with new ones. The technician is coming in on Monday to begin work. The librarian is ordering new reference materials. They're going to be here by next semester.

We're going to expand our recycling program. I'm meeting with some people from the environmental studies program this afternoon to finalize the details.

The biggest news is that we're building a new student center. It's going to have a food court, a large bookstore, and conference rooms for student groups to meet in. We think that the builders are going to start next week. Unfortunately, it isn't going to be ready until next year.

I hope you're looking forward to the great new services on campus! Thank you, once again, for all of your help!

Exercise 3.3: Pronunciation Focus: Information Questions with *Will*
(p. 344 / track 43)

When people speak quickly and informally, they often use the contraction *'ll* instead of *will* after a *Wh-* word.	***Who'll*** *turn garbage into energy?* ***What'll*** *we do without oil?* ***How'll*** *we use body heat to warm a building?* ***When'll*** *we have cleaner cars and trucks?*

A (p. 344 / track 44)

Who'll turn garbage into energy?
What'll we do without oil?
How'll we use body heat to warm a building?
When'll we have cleaner cars and trucks?

Unit 28

Exercise 2.1: *Will, May,* and *Might*

A (p. 351 / track 45)

Carla	So what're your plans for the fall? Are you going to college?
Sharon	Actually, I might not go to a college. But I think I'll probably enroll in an online program.
Carla	Oh, really? Like a degree online?
Sharon	Yeah, or maybe just a few courses. The thing is that my family is definitely going to move this year. So with an online program, I probably won't need to change schools.
Carla	That's smart. You can study from anywhere. Do you know what you're going to take?
Sharon	I think so. I like chemistry, so I'll definitely take chemistry.
Carla	Oh, so you're interested in science?
Sharon	Yeah. And I might take biology, too. I'll definitely take Spanish.
Carla	Awesome! But why Spanish?
Sharon	Well, my family's going to move to California, so I thought Spanish might be useful.
Carla	Well, let me know how it goes.
Sharon	Sure. I'll definitely keep in touch. I'll be online all the time!

Unit 29

Exercise 2.2: More Suggestions and Advice

A (p. 364 / track 46)

Professor	Taking good notes is an important part of being a successful student. Let's hear some advice from students about how they take notes.
Teresa	Some teachers speak very quickly. You should ask these teachers if you can record the class. Then you can listen to the notes again in your home. You shouldn't record the class without the teacher's permission.
Amadou	You might want to attend a workshop on note taking. That can be very helpful. I know it helped me.
Alex	Find a student with good notes and ask him or her if you can copy the notes. You should probably offer to buy that student coffee or a snack. Maybe you should suggest a time to meet once a week to trade notes. If you aren't sure how to suggest this, here are some ways: "Why don't we get together on Thursdays to trade notes?" or "Let's meet in the student union."
Professor	Thank you for your suggestions. I ought to add here that you shouldn't just copy the notes. You should compare their notes with yours. Try to figure out what's different.

Unit 30

Exercise 2.2: Pronunciation Focus: *Have To* and *Has To*

(p. 377 / track 47)

Have to is usually pronounced "hafta."	I **hafta** win the game. You **hafta** see my new game!
Has to is usually pronounced "hasta."	She **hasta** try harder to win. He **hasta** think quickly when he plays this game!

A (p. 377 / track 48)

I hafta win the game.
You hafta see my new game!
She hasta try harder to win.
He hasta think quickly when he plays this game!

B (p. 378 / track 49)

Welcome to the Stack'em game website! Here are some tips on how to win the game!

1. You don't have to know many rules to win the game.
2. A player has to move around different shapes to make lines.
3. Players have to turn the pieces to make them fit.
4. The pieces have to fit together with no spaces to make the line disappear.
5. As players get better, the pieces come more quickly. The player has to think very quickly.
6. You don't have to play against someone. You can play by yourself.
7. Players have to have one of the top five scores for their name to be added to the "champion" list.
8. Stack'em is fantastic! You have to play a lot to become good, but it's fun!

Unit 31

Exercise 3.2: Adjectives with *Very* and *Too*

B (p. 392 / track 50)

1. The party lasted for six hours. The party was very long, so we went home early.
2. The party lasted for an hour. Everyone wanted to stay longer. The party was too short.
3. There were 75 people at the party. The living room holds 50. The room was too small.
4. There were five people at the table. The table seats 12. The table was too big.
5. The party was noisy, and I couldn't hear conversations. The party was too noisy.
6. The party was noisy, but I had a great time. The party was very noisy.
7. Some people spoke quickly, but I understood most of it. Some people spoke very quickly.
8. One man spoke quickly, and I didn't understand a word of it. He spoke too quickly.

9. It was 25° F (-4° C) outside on the porch. We had to leave. It was too cold.
10. It was 43° F (6° C) outside on the porch. I wore my coat. It was very cold.

Unit 32

Exercise 3.1: Making Comparisons with Adverbs
(p. 406 / track 51)

Joe	Hi, Bill. Are you home for the summer?
Bill	Yes, Joe, I'm back from college. It's really nice to be back in Grant.
Joe	Are you kidding? It's so boring here. Didn't you like living in New York City?
Bill	Well, yes, I did. But the lifestyle is so different.
Joe	What do you mean?
Bill	Well, it seems like everyone is always in a rush. People walk more quickly, and they even talk faster. They work harder, and their hours are longer. People seem more serious.
Joe	But you're a student. The city is a fun place to be a student, isn't it?
Bill	Yes, it is. Restaurants and clubs stay open later, and there's so much to do. But everything is more expensive than it is in Grant, so you have to choose carefully to find some inexpensive places. On the weekends, I went out more often than I do here.
Joe	Yeah. In Grant, you have to drive further to get to a mall or movie. It takes an hour to get to the movie theater. But the good thing is – because there's nothing to do, we go out less often, so we spend money more slowly.
Bill	That's for sure. And that's a good thing because this summer I need to get a job and save money for next year in New York City!

Unit 33

Exercise 2.2: Superlative Adjectives to Describe People
B (p. 418 / track 52)

Claire	So, who are the most important people in your life?
Monika	Well, I guess my family and my best friends.
Claire	OK. Tell me about your family.
Monika	Well, let's see. My closest family members all live near me, so I see them often. I have three brothers: Tim, Liam, and Anthony. Anthony is the youngest. He's just 13. My grandmother is 75. She's my oldest relative. My friends are mostly from my college days. One really special person is Tina.
Claire	Tina? Is she your best friend?
Monika	Yeah. She's the most unusual person I know, and the most interesting. She has a pilot's license and a degree in biology! Of all my friends, she definitely has the most exciting job. She works for a tour company that takes people to some of the most exotic places in the world. When we were in college, she always got the highest grades. She's probably the most intelligent person I know, and the most successful.
Claire	Amazing!

Answer Key

1 Statements with Present of *Be*
Tell Me About Yourself

1 Grammar in the Real World

A page 2

Answers will vary.

B Comprehension Check page 3

1. an adviser
2. South Korea
3. store

C Notice page 3

1. 'm; 'm
2. is
3. are; 're.

2 Present of *Be*: Affirmative Statements
Exercise 2.1 Present of *Be*: Full Forms

A page 5

2. are	5. are
3. is	6. is
4. is	7. are

B page 5

2. It	5. He
3. They	6. He
4. She	7. We

C page 6

2. am	7. are
3. are	8. am
4. am	9. are
5. am	10. is
6. is	

D Over to You page 6

1. is; *Answers will vary.*
2. am; *Answers will vary.*
3. am; *Answers will vary.*
4. is; *Answers will vary.*
5. is; *Answers will vary.*
6. am; *Answers will vary.*
7. *Answers will vary.*

Exercise 2.2 Present of *Be*: Contractions

A pages 6–7

2. 's	10. 's
3. 's	11. 're
4. 'm	12. 're
5. 's	13. 's
6. 're	14. 's
7. 're	15. 'm
8. 's	16. 's
9. 's	

B Pair Work page 7

Answers will vary.

3 Present of *Be*: Negative Statements
Exercise 3.1 Present of *Be*: Negative Statements with Full Forms

A page 8

2. are not	6. am not
3. is not	7. is not
4. are not	8. are not
5. is not	

B Over to You page 9

2. am not; *Answers will vary.*
3. am not; *Answers will vary.*
4. am not; *Answers will vary.*
5. am not; *Answers will vary.*
6. am not; *Answers will vary.*

C Pair Work page 9

Answers will vary.

Exercise 3.2 Affirmative or Negative?

A page 9

2. aren't / are not
3. is; isn't / 's not
4. isn't / 's not; 's
5. is; isn't / 's not
6. aren't / 're not
7. 're; aren't / 're not
8. isn't
9. isn't
10. is; isn't

B page 10

2. are; They're not / They aren't
3. are; They're not / They aren't
4. They're not / They aren't; They're
5. He's not / He isn't; He's
6. They're not / They aren't; They're

C Pair Work page 10

Answers will vary.

Exercise 3.3 Negative of Be pages 10–11

2. 's not
3. isn't
4. 's not
5. 're not
6. 're not
7. 're not

4 Avoid Common Mistakes

Editing Task page 11

2. Her name is Amy.
3. Amy and I are roommates.
4. She's / She is 27.
5. She isn't / is not a student.
6. She's / She is a science teacher.
7. She's / She is very nice and very smart.
8. Amy isn't / is not in school today.
9. She's / She is sick.
10. She's / She is at home.

5 Grammar for Writing

Writing About a Person

Pre-writing Task

1 page 12

The writer's sister is the important person.

2 page 12

My sister(is)an important person in my life. Her name(is)
Lila. She(is)23 years old. She(is)a nurse at Cottage Hospital.
Her interests(are)dancing and music. She(is not)interested
in sports. She(is)tall. Her hair(is)long, and she(is)very
beautiful. She(is)also very funny. She(is)still single. She and I
(are)good friends. We(are)together often.
The verb *be* appears 13 times in the paragraph.

Writing Task

1 Write page 12

Answers will vary.

2 Self-Edit page 13

Answers will vary.

2 Yes / No Questions and Information Questions with *Be*

Schedules and School

1 Grammar in the Real World

A page 14

Answers will vary; Possible answer: Yuko and Juan have the
same reading class on Mondays.

B Comprehension Check page 15

1. False
2. False
3. True
4. True

C Notice page 15

1. Are
2. Is
3. Is
4. Are

Verbs are at the beginning of the questions.

2 Yes / No Questions and Short Answers with *Be*

Exercise 2.1 Singular Yes / No Questions
and Answers

A page 17

2. Are; I'm not
3. Are; I am
4. Is; he / she is
5. Are; I'm not
6. Is; he / she isn't
7. Is; it is
8. Is; it isn't

B page 18

1. b. Is she at home?   No, she isn't.
2. a. Is he hungry?   Yes, he is.
   b. Is he at the store?   No, he isn't.
3. a. Is it / the library open? No, it isn't.
   b. Is it a white building?   No, it isn't.

Exercise 2.2 Plural Yes / No Questions
and Answers page 18

John: Are you and your classmates happy?
Eric: Yes, we are.
John: Are the homework assignments easy?
Eric: No, they aren't / are not.
John: Are your classmates on time?
Eric: No, they aren't / are not.
John: Are you and your friends busy?
Eric: Yes, we are.
John: Are the exams difficult?
Eric: Yes, they are.

Exercise 2.3 Singular and Plural *Yes / No* Questions and Answers page 19

2. Are they from the same country? No, they aren't / are not.
3. Are they good students? Yes, they are.
4. Is Paulo smart? Yes, he is.
5. Is Paulo lazy? No, he isn't / is not.
6. Are Julio's classes every day from Monday to Friday? No, they aren't / are not.

3 Information Questions with *Be*

Exercise 3.1 Information Questions with *Be*

A page 21

2. Where's   4. Who's
3. What's   5. When's

B page 21

2. How old are   4. How many; are
3. How much is   5. How much are

Exercise 3.2 Information Questions and Answers page 22

2. What is the student's name? It's / It is Jason Armenio.
3. When is the spring semester? It's / It is February 1 through May 28.
4. What is his major? It's / It is history.
5. How much is the tuition? It's / It is $600.
6. How much is the parking permit? It's / It is $20.
7. What is the total? It's / It is $637.
8. When are the final exams? They're / They are May 24 through 28.

Exercise 3.3 More Information Questions and Answers

Pair Work page 22

Answers will vary.

4 Avoid Common Mistakes

Editing Task page 23

2. What is the school's name~~:~~ **?**
3. How much *is* the tuition ~~is~~?
4. *Is* "~~your~~ your school expensive~~:~~ **?**" "Yes, ~~it's~~ *it is*."
5. What *'s / is* ~~your~~ your major?
6. *Are* ~~Is~~ you a good student?

7. When *is* summer break ~~is~~?
8. *Are* ~~Is~~ all your classes difficult?

5 Grammar for Writing

Using Questions to Get Information About a Topic

Pre-writing Task

1 page 24

No answers.

2 pages 24–25

2. is your school
3. is your major
4. are your business classes
5. is your first language
6. is your birthday
7. are your interests
8. Are you
9. is your wife's name
10. Is she

Writing Task

1 Write page 25

Answers will vary.

2 Self-Edit page 25

Answers will vary.

3 Count Nouns; *A / An*; *Have* and *Be*
Gadgets

1 Grammar in the Real World

A page 26

Answers will vary.

B Comprehension Check page 27

1. No
2. Yes
3. Yes

C Notice page 27

1. an
2. a
3. hours
4. phone

2 Nouns; *A / An*

Exercise 2.1 *A* or *An*

A page 28

2. an	7. an
3. a	8. a
4. a	9. a
5. a	10. a
6. a	

B Over to You page 29

Answers will vary.

Exercise 2.2 Plural Nouns

A page 29

batteries; calculators; cell phones; computers; video cameras
dictionaries; notebooks
Accessories; dresses; belts; purses

B Pair Work page 29

Answers will vary.

Exercise 2.3 Pronunciation Focus: Plural Nouns

A page 30

1. ☐
2. ☐
3. ☐
4. ☐
5. ☑
6. ☐
7. ☑
8. ☐
9. ☐

Nouns with an extra syllable in the plural form: items 5, 7

B page 30

	Yes	No
2. taxes	☑	☐
3. CD players	☐	☑
4. cases	☑	☐
5. oranges	☑	☐
6. pennies	☐	☑
7. students	☐	☑
8. brushes	☑	☐
9. dictionaries	☐	☑
10. matches	☑	☐
11. chairs	☐	☑
12. quizzes	☑	☐
13. pens	☐	☑
14. garages	☑	☐

Exercise 2.4 Proper Nouns page 30

Answers will vary.

3 *Be* with *A / An* + Noun

Exercise 3.1 *A / An* + Noun page 31

2. an	7. an
3. a	8. a
4. an	9. an
5. a	10. a
6. a	11. a

Exercise 3.2 *A / An* + Noun: Occupations

A page 32

2. a	2. is a chef.
3. b	3. is an electrician.
4. d	4. are mechanics.
5. e	5. is a pharmacist.
6. f	6. are receptionists.

B Over to You page 33

Answers will vary.

4 *Have*

Exercise 4.1 *Have* page 34

2. has	6. has
3. has	7. has
4. has	8. have
5. have	

Exercise 4.2 *Have* and *Be* page 34

2. is	10. has
3. is	11. have
4. has	12. are
5. has	13. have
6. is	14. is
7. is	15. is
8. am	16. are
9. is	

5 Avoid Common Mistakes

Editing Task page 35

2. My neighbors ~~is~~ *are* very friendly.

3. Tom and Nancy Lim ~~is~~ *are* my neighbors.

4. Nancy is *a* computer programmer.

5. Tom is *a* cell phone designer.

6. Their children ~~is~~ *are* Joe and Cathy.

7. Joe and Cathy ~~is~~ *are* students at Hatfield College.

8. Joe is *a* student in the computer department.

9. He ~~have~~ *has* a lot of classes this year.

10. Cathy is *a* busy architecture student.

6 Grammar for Writing

Writing About a Favorite Place

Pre-writing Task

1 page 36

You can visit monuments, the Pyramids, museums, parks, and the subway system.

2 page 36

I <u>have</u> a favorite <u>city</u>. The city (is Giza), Egypt. It <u>has</u> a lot of beautiful <u>monuments</u>. It also <u>has</u> a lot of <u>museums and</u> beautiful <u>parks</u>. My favorite park (is Orman Park). Gizza <u>has</u> a fast and clean <u>subway system</u>.

Writing Task

1 Write page 37

Answers will vary.

2 Self-Edit page 37

Answers will vary.

4 Demonstratives and Possessives

The Workplace

1 Grammar in the Real World

A page 38

Answers will vary; Possible answer: The speakers mention 11 things: a desk, closet, office supplies, cabinets, printers, copy machines, papers, drawers, photographs, conference rooms, and reports.

B Comprehension Check page 39

1. c   2. e   3. b   4. a   5. d

C Notice page 39

1. these
2. That
3. Those
4. this

Before singular nouns: that, this
Before plural nouns: these, those

2 Demonstratives (*This, That, These, Those*)

Exercise 2.1 Demonstratives with Singular and Plural Nouns page 42

2. That   7. These
3. Those   8. That
4. This   9. That
5. These   10. These
6. That

Exercise 2.2 More Demonstratives with Singular and Plural Nouns

Pair Work page 42

Answers will vary.

Exercise 2.3 Demonstratives without Nouns

A page 43

3. ~~thing~~
4. ~~model~~
5. ~~model~~
6. the new model ✓
7. ~~headphones~~

B page 43

Same as **A**.

Exercise 2.4 Questions and Answers with Demonstratives page 43

1. that; It's
2. these; They're
3. this; It's
4. those; They're
5. these; They're; They're
6. that; It's

Exercise 2.5 More Questions and Answers with Demonstratives

Pair Work page 44

Answers will vary.

Exercise 2.6 Vocabulary Focus: Responses with *That's* page 44

Possible answers:

2. That's great.   5. That's wonderful.
3. That's too bad.   6. That's good.
4. That's terrible.

3 Possessives and *Whose*

Exercise 3.1 Possessives page 47

2. our
3. your
4. my
5. her
6. Juliana's
7. Their
8. our
9. His
10. Mr. Donovan's

Exercise 3.2 Possessive *'s or s'*?

A pages 47–48

2. Krista's
3. managers'
4. Sara's
5. brothers'
6. Tom's
7. daughter's
8. cats'

B Pair Work page 48

Answers will vary.

Exercise 3.3 Questions with *Whose* and *Who's*

A page 48

2. Whose; Ki-woon's birthday is in June.
3. Who's; Ling is Chinese.
4. Whose; Ki-woon's major is Business.
5. Who's; Missolle is Haitian.
6. Who's; Ki-woon is from South Korea.
7. Whose; Ling's major is Nursing.
8. Whose; Ling's birthday is in October.
9. Who's; Ki-woon is interested in soccer.
10. Whose; Missolle's interests are music and cooking.

B Pair Work page 48

Answers will vary.

4 Avoid Common Mistakes

Editing Task page 49

A: Hi. I'm sorry to interrupt you, but where's the manager͗s office?

B: ~~Its~~ *It's* next to Claudia͗s *'s* office.

A: Where is ~~those~~ *that*? I don't know Claudia.

B: Oh, it's down ~~these~~ *this* hallway right here. Turn left after you pass ~~that~~ *those* two elevators.

A: Oh, OK. You mean ~~its~~ *it's* near the two assistants͗ office.

B: That's right. Do you know them?

A: Yes, I do.

B: Then please give them a message. ~~Theirs~~ *Their* folders are on my desk.

5 Grammar for Writing
Writing About Things and People's Possessions

Pre-writing Task

1 page 50

The writer describes the people on her new team.

2 page 50

Hi Jun,

How are you? How is (your) new job? This is a picture of the people at the office. It is (our) new team. That is (your) friend Jung Won in the front. She's married now. Those two men in the back are new. (Their) names are Francisco and Jack. They are (Casey's) friends. (Paula's) new roommate, Sandy, is on (our) team, too. Pietro and Diego are not in this office anymore. (Their) office is downtown.
Let's talk soon.
Alexia

The writer uses *our* to refer to the team she and Jung were a part of and which Alexia is still a part of.

Writing Task

1 Write page 51

Answers will vary.

2 Self-Edit page 51

Answers will vary.

5 Descriptive Adjectives
Skills and Qualities for Success

1 Grammar in the Real World

A page 52

Answers will vary; Possible answer: Yes, these websites are useful for employers.

B Comprehension Check page 52

Possible answers:
1. JobsLink is a social networking website.
2. Julia is a student.
3. Ricardo is an employer.
4. Julia has an interview with Ricardo.

C Notice page 53

1. It's like a (big) bulletin board.
2. He has a (small) business.
3. Julia is a (hardworking) student at a (large) community college.
4. Julia has a (new) job.
The adjectives come before the nouns.

2 Adjectives

Exercise 2.1 Adjective + Noun

A page 54

2. James is a hardworking person.
3. This is a useful website.
4. It has interesting jobs.
5. This is a large company.
6. James can send his new résumé.

B page 55

Answers will vary.

Exercise 2.2 Vocabulary Focus: Opposites with Adjective + Noun and *Be* + Adjective

A page 55

2. new
3. small
4. tall
5. good
6. long

B Pair Work page 55

Answers will vary.

C page 56

2. long
3. happy
4. interesting
5. old
6. young
7. friendly / helpful
8. helpful / friendly
9. late

Exercise 2.3 Vocabulary Focus: Nationality Adjectives

A page 57

2. Chilean
3. Kuwaiti
4. German
5. Vietnamese
6. English

B Over to You page 57

Answers will vary.

3 Questions with *What . . . like?* and *How* + Adjective

Exercise 3.1 Questions with *What . . . like?*

A page 58

2. It's an old Midwestern city in Missouri.
3. What's; like
4. It's very cold, and it's snowy.
5. What are; like
6. They're very friendly.
7. What are; like
8. They're good and not too expensive.

B page 58

Same as **A**.

C Over to You page 58

Answers will vary.

Exercise 3.2 Questions with *How* + Adjective

A page 59

2. How hot
3. How cold
4. How crowded
5. How expensive
6. How bad

B Pair Work page 59

Answers will vary.

4 Avoid Common Mistakes

Editing Task page 60

My name is Enrique. I'm ~~brazilian~~ *Brazilian*. My company is called SoftPro. It's a ~~company new~~ *new company*. We have 25 ~~excellents~~ *excellent* employees. We have ~~a~~ *an* ambitious plan for accounting software. I want to find more ~~smarts~~ *smart* people to work at SoftPro.

My name is Yuko. I *am* Japanese. I'm a saleswoman in ~~an~~ *a* Japanese computer company. It's a ~~company big~~ *big company*. We have many ~~importants~~ *important* customers in Japan and South Korea. However, most of our customers are ~~chinese~~ *Chinese*.

5 Grammar for Writing
Writing About Skills and Qualities

Pre-writing Task

1 page 61

The writer describes eight qualities.

2 page 61

My 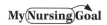Nursing Goal

My goal is to be a nurse for young children. I have a lot of useful qualities for nursing. I am a very friendly person. I love people, and I am very good with young children and small babies. I am also patient. I am a very hard-working person, and I am strong. My communication skills are good. I am smart. My science class grades are high. These qualities are very important for successful nurses.

The writer uses *very* with *friendly*, *good*, *hard-working*, and *important*. She uses it to make her statements stronger.

Writing Task

1 Write page 61

Answers will vary.

2 Self-Edit page 61

Answers will vary.

6 Prepositions
Around the House

1 Grammar in the Real World

A page 62

Answers will vary.

B Comprehension Check page 63

1. b   2. d   3. a   4. c   5. e

C Notice page 63

1. in
2. on top of
3. on; next to
4. on
5. at
Something happens: items 4, 5
Where something is: items 1, 2, 3

2 Prepositions of Place: Things at Home and in the Neighborhood
Exercise 2.1 Prepositions of Place: Things at Home

A page 65

Possible answer:
2. in front of the refrigerator
3. under the table
4. on top of your gym bag
5. on top of the refrigerator
6. behind the door
7. on the counter
8. in the coffee maker

B page 65

Possible answers:
2. Where's / Where is his watch? It's on the table.
3. Where are his glasses? They're on / on top of the coffee machine.
4. Where are his headphones? They're under a chair.
5. Where's / Where is his notebook? It's under the books.

C Pair Work page 66

Answers will vary.

Exercise 2.2 Prepositions of Place: Things in the Neighborhood

A page 66

2. The camera store is between the shoe store and the coffee shop.
3. The red car is at the gas station.
4. The shopping carts are outside / in front of the supermarket.
5. The bookstore is next to the bank.

B page 67

2. above the coffee shop.
3. across from the supermarket.
4. next to the school.
5. across from the school.

C Pair Work page 67

Answers will vary.

3 Prepositions of Place: Locations and Other Uses
Exercise 3.1 *In*, *On*, and *At* with Locations

A Pair Work page 68

1. in; *Answers will vary.*
2. in; *Answers will vary.*

3. on; *Answers will vary.*
4. at; *Answers will vary.*
5. on; *Answers will vary.*
6. on; *Answers will vary.*

B page 69

2. in	7. on
3. in	8. in
4. at	9. on
5. at	10. in
6. on	11. in

Exercise 3.2 *In*, *On*, and *At* with Locations and Ordinal Numbers

A Over to You page 69

2. *Answers will vary.*
3. in; *Answers will vary.*
4. on; *Answers will vary.*
5. at; *Answers will vary.*
6. *Answers will vary.*
7. on; the; *Answers will vary.*
8. *Answers will vary.*

B Pair Work page 69

Answers will vary.

Exercise 3.3 Expressions with *In*, *On*, and *At* page 70

1. at; at; at / in; on
2. in; on; in; at / in
3. in; on; at; at
4. in; at / in; at / in; on

4 Prepositions of Time

Exercise 4.1 *In*, *On*, *At* with Time

A page 72

1. in; in	5. in
2. in	6. at
3. in	7. on
4. in	8. at; in

B page72

2. between	7. at / around
3. on	8. on
4. on	9. on
5. in	10. at / around
6. at	

C Over to You page 72

Answers will vary.

Exercise 4.2 Questions with Days, Dates, and Times

A page 73

2. What day is the concert?
3. When do the students have a break?
4. What day is the Career Fair?
5. When is lunch?
6. What time is the welcome?

B Pair Work page 73

Possible answers:
2. It's on Friday, April 23rd.
3. They have a break between 11:15 and 11:30.
4. It's on Friday, April 23rd.
5. It's from 12:30 to 1:30.
6. It's at 9:00.

5 Avoid Common Mistakes

Editing Task page 74

Hi everyone,

I have some news and an invitation! Vikram turns 25 years old ~~on~~ *in* September, and I want to have a party for him. Unfortunately, his birthday is ~~in~~ *on* September 2, and that's ~~in~~ *on* Monday. Many of us have to work on that day, so let's have his party ~~in~~ *on* August 31. That's ~~in~~ *on* Saturday.

Let's all meet at my apartment *at* 7:00 ~~in~~ *on* Saturday. I can invite Vikram to my apartment, too, and we can surprise him. Then we can take him to his favorite restaurant. There's a great Spanish restaurant ~~at~~ *on* Grand Avenue. I hope you can all come. My apartment is ~~on~~ *at* 8 Bryant Place. I live ~~in~~ *on the* third floor.

Thanks,

Alyssa

6 Grammar for Writing

Using Prepositions

Pre-writing Task

1 page 75

The invitation is for a graduation party. The party is on Saturday, the ninth, from 6:00 p.m. until midnight. It's at 616 Campana Way.

2 page 75

Hi Raul,

You're invited (to) a graduation party (for) Claudia (at) my house (on) Saturday, the ninth. The party is (at) 6:00 p.m. I have a new apartment. It's (at) 616 Campana Way. My apartment is (on) the third floor. My building doesn't have a parking lot. You can park (in) the parking lot (behind) the bank. The bank is (across from) the gas station (on) Kellogg Street.

Daniel

What: A graduation party for Claudia When: Saturday, the ninth, from 6:00 p.m. until midnight Where: 616 Campana Way, third floor

Writing Task

1 Write page 75

Answers will vary.

2 Self-Edit page 75

Answers will vary.

7 *There Is* and *There Are*
Local Attractions

1 Grammar in the Real World

A page 76

Answers will vary; Possible answer: Some fun things to do: See historic buildings, see statues, shop, visit restaurants, listen to traditional music, and watch folk dancing.

B Comprehension Check page 77

1. e   2. d   3. b   4. a   5. c

C Notice page 77

There is ...	There are ...
traditional music	27 historic buildings, restaurants
a statue of King Carlos III	a lot of interesting things to do

There is; There are

2 *There Is / There Are*
Exercise 2.1 Affirmative Statements

A page 79

2. There are
3. there's
4. there's
5. there's
6. there's
7. There's
8. There are
9. There are

B Over to You page 80

Answers will vary.

C Pair Work page 80

Answers will vary.

Exercise 2.2 Affirmative and Negative Statements

A page 80

3. There isn't
4. There aren't
5. There isn't
6. There aren't
7. There is
8. There aren't
9. There is
10. There is

B Over to You page 81

Answers will vary.

Exercise 2.3 *There Is / There Are* or *It is / They Are*

A pages 81–82

3. There are
4. They're
5. There's
6. It's
7. It's
8. There are
9. There's
10. There's
11. It's
12. There are
13. there's

B page 82

Same as **A**.

C Over to You page 82

Answers will vary.

3 Yes / No Questions with *There Is / There Are*
Exercise 3.1 Questions and Answers

A page 84

1. Are there any; are
2. Is there a; there's / there is
3. Are there any; are; 1:00 a.m.; 2:00 a.m.
4. Are there any; No, there aren't.
5. Is there a; There's / There is
6. Are there any; No, there aren't.
7. Is there a; Yes, there is.
8. Is there a; Yes, there is.

B Pair Work page 84

1. Is there an art festival?; *Answers will vary.*
2. Are there any jazz concerts?; *Answers will vary.*
3. Is there a baseball game?; *Answers will vary.*
4. Is there a dance performance?; *Answers will vary.*
5. Are there any new paintings at the museum?; *Answers will vary.*
6. Are there any good movies?; *Answers will vary.*

C page 85

Answers will vary.

4 Avoid Common Mistakes

Editing Task page 86

    New York City is an expensive place to visit, but there
is
~~are~~ one place that is always free: Central Park. ~~There~~ *It* is a

very big park. In fact, it is about 2.5 miles (4 km) long and
are
0.5 miles (0.8 km) wide. There ~~is~~ over 843 acres in the park.
are
There ~~is~~ fields, ponds, and lakes. Visitors enjoy different

kinds of sports and events here. There are walkers, joggers,
There is
skaters, bicyclists, and bird-watchers. ~~There's~~ a zoo and
There is
two ice-skating rinks. ~~There's~~ also an outdoor theater. The

theater has "Shakespeare in the Park" summer festivals.

There is a swimming pool in the summer, too. Throughout
there are
the year, ~~they're~~ horse and carriage rides. Every year, there
are
~~is~~ over 25 million visitors. They are happy to visit a fun and

free New York City tourist attraction.

5 Grammar for Writing
Writing About Places

Pre-writing Task

1 page 87

The writer describes a big park near his / her apartment.
There is a playground, some small lakes, a fountain, and
picnic tables.

2 page 87

    There is a big park near my apartment. It is very

beautiful. There is a playground in the park. It always has

a lot of children. There are also some small lakes. One

lake is for swimming. It has a little beach. The

other lakes do not have any beaches. They are for

fishing. There are some small boats to rent. There is a

fountain in the center of the park. It is a very cool place

to be in the summer. There are not any food stands, but

there are a lot of picnic tables.

Writing Task

1 Write page 87

Answers will vary.

2 Self-Edit page 87

Answers will vary.

8 Simple Present
Lifestyles

1 Grammar in the Real World

A page 88

Answers will vary; Possible answer: They live a lifestyle that
is common for people who have a long life.

B Comprehension Check page 89

Possible answers:
1. People live so long because of their lifestyle.
2. They rarely feel stressed.
3. They usually don't eat much meat.

C Notice page 89

1. move
2. don't
3. walk
4. Every day; take

don't: 2
time: every day

2 Simple Present: Affirmative and Negative Statements
Exercise 2.1 Simple Present Statements
page 91

2. goes
3. checks; works
4. is
5. works
6. does
7. relax
8. eat; don't / do not smoke

Exercise 2.2 More Simple Present Statements
page 92

2. feel
3. works
4. doesn't / does not see
5. take
6. don't / do not have
7. eat
8. doesn't / does not have
9. goes
10. runs
11. relax

Exercise 2.3 More Simple Present Statements

A Over to You page 92

Possible answers:
1. don't / do not feel *OR* feel
2. don't / do not have *OR* have
3. don't / do not live *OR* live
4. don't / do not exercise *OR* exercise
5. don't / do not eat *OR* eat
6. don't / do not sleep *OR* sleep
7. don't / do not spend *OR* spend
8. don't / do not do *OR* do
9. don't / do not drink *OR* drink
10. don't / do not read *OR* read

B Pair Work page 93

Answers will vary.

Exercise 2.4 Pronunciation Focus: -s and -es

A page 93

No answers.

B page 93

Staci <u>goes</u> to school from Monday to Friday from 7:30 a.m. to 11:30 a.m. Then she <u>rushes</u> to work. She <u>works</u> at a hospital until 8:00 p.m. In the evening, Staci <u>catches</u> a bus to go home. On her way home, she <u>listens</u> to music and <u>relaxes</u>. She <u>eats</u> a quick dinner with her family. Then she <u>reads</u> to her children and <u>checks</u> their homework. If she isn't too tired, she <u>finishes</u> her own homework. Staci usually <u>falls</u> asleep by 10:00 p.m.

C page 94

	/s/	/z/	/əz/
2. rushes			✓
3. works	✓		
4. catches			✓
5. listens		✓	
6. relaxes			✓
7. eats	✓		
8. reads		✓	
9. checks	✓		
10. finishes			✓
11. falls		✓	

D Pair Work page 94

Answers will vary.

Exercise 2.5 Using Time Expressions with Simple Present

A page 95

3. from 7:30 a.m. to 2:30 p.m.
4. on Tuesdays and Thursdays
5. from 7:15 p.m. to 9:45 p.m.
6. Saturdays and Sundays
7. on Sundays
8. at 11:00 p.m.; at 6:30 a.m.
9. on Saturdays

B Over to You page 95

Answers will vary.

3 Statements with Adverbs of Frequency

Exercise 3.1 Adverbs of Frequency with Simple Present page 97

2. He often does not listen to music.
3. He never slows down.
4. He sometimes works seven days a week.
5. He rarely takes a day off.
6. He usually starts work at 3:00 in the afternoon.
7. He usually doesn't finish until 1:00 a.m.
8. My brother is rarely tired.

Exercise 3.2 More Adverbs of Frequency with Simple Present

A Over to You page 98

Answers will vary.

B Pair Work page 98

Answers will vary.

4 Avoid Common Mistakes

Editing Task page 99

Dear Pedro,

How are you? I'm fine. I'm in Vermont with my aunt and uncle. They ~~lives~~ *live* on a farm. The lifestyle here is very different. They are dairy farmers, so they ~~are~~ work hard every day. They usually get up at 4:30 a.m. They go to the barn and milk the cows.

Cows ~~makes~~ *make* a lot of noise in the morning, so they usually ~~wakes~~ *wake* me up. Of course, I do not ~~gets~~ *get* up until about 7:00 a.m. At 9:00, my uncle ~~cook~~ *cooks* a wonderful breakfast. We all eat together. After that, he and I ~~goes~~ *go* to the barn and ~~works~~ *work* there. My aunt usually stays ~~stay~~ *stays* in the house. In the afternoon, there is more work. At night, I am really tired, so I always ~~goes~~ *go* to bed at 8:30! Usually my aunt and uncle ~~don't be~~ *aren't / are not* tired. They usually go to bed late!

I hope your vacation is fun. See you soon!

Your friend,

Oscar

5 Grammar for Writing
Writing About Daily Life

Pre-writing Task

1 page 100

The routines happen at night. The writer's husband goes to bed early and wakes up early; the writer goes to bed late and gets up late.

2 page 100

My husband and I <u>have</u> very different routines. My husband (usually) <u>goes</u> to bed early. (Sometimes) he <u>watches</u> TV and then <u>goes</u> to bed around 9:00. I (never) <u>go</u> to bed early. I (usually) <u>check</u> my e-mail. I (often) <u>surf</u> the Internet. I (never) <u>watch</u> TV, but I (sometimes) <u>read</u>. Then, around midnight, I <u>drink</u> some warm milk and <u>go</u> to sleep. My husband (always) <u>gets up</u> early. He <u>goes</u> for a run, and then he <u>makes</u> coffee. When the coffee <u>is</u> ready, I <u>get</u> up.

The writer's routines	The writer's husband's routines
never goes to bed early	goes to bed early
checks e-mail	watches TV
surfs the Internet	goes to bed around 9:00
never watches TV	gets up early
reads	goes for a run
drinks warm milk and goes to sleep	makes coffee
gets up when coffee is ready	

Writing Task

1 Write page 101

Answers will vary.

2 Self-Edit page 101

Answers will vary.

9 Simple Present *Yes / No* Questions and Short Answers
Daily Habits

1 Grammar in the Real World

A page 102

Answers will vary.

B Comprehension Check page 102

1. sleep
2. work
3. health problems

C Notice page 103

1. Do most <u>people</u> get enough sleep?
2. Do <u>you</u> suffer from insomnia
3. Does <u>stress</u> keep you awake?

Singular subjects use *do*; plural subjects use *does*.

2 Simple Present *Yes / No* Questions and Short Answers
Exercise 2.1 *Yes / No* Questions and Short Answers

A page 104

2. Does; Yes, it does. OR No, it doesn't.
3. Does; Yes, it does. OR No, it doesn't.
4. Do; Yes, I do. OR No, I don't.
5. Do; Yes, I do. OR No, I don't.
6. Do; Yes, I do. OR No, I don't.
7. Do; Yes, I do. OR No, I don't.
8. Do; Yes, I do. OR No, I don't.

B Pair Work page 105

Answers will vary.

Exercise 2.2 More *Yes / No* Questions and Short Answers

A page 105

Conversation 1
2. we don't
3. does your brother do
4. he does
5. Does he work
6. he doesn't
7. Does he go
8. he doesn't

Conversation 2
1. Do your grandparents live
2. they do
3. Do you and your family see
4. we don't
5. Do they need
6. they don't
7. Do they visit
8. they don't

B Pair Work page 105

No answers.

Exercise 2.3 Pronunciation Focus: *Do you . . . ?*

A page 106

No answers.

B Pair Work page 106

Answers will vary.

Exercise 2.4 *Yes / No* Questions in a Survey

A Over to You page 106

2. Do you fall asleep to music?; *Answers will vary.*
3. Do you talk in your sleep?; *Answers will vary.*
4. Do you dream a lot?; *Answers will vary.*
5. Do you remember your dreams?; *Answers will vary.*
6. Do you walk in your sleep?; *Answers will vary.*
7. Do you hit the "snooze" button 2 or 3 times?; *Answers will vary.*
8. Do you get enough sleep?; *Answers will vary.*

B Pair Work page 107

Answers will vary.

3 Avoid Common Mistakes

Editing Task page 107

2. ~~Are~~ *Do* you sleep on your stomach, your back, or your side?
3. ~~Have you~~ *Do you have* a TV in your bedroom?
4. ~~Does~~ *Do* you dream in color or in black-and-white?

5. ~~Do~~ *Does* a dream ever scare you?
6. ~~Does~~ *Do* loud noises wake you up at night?
7. ~~Do~~ *Are* you a light sleeper or a deep sleeper?
8. ~~Does~~ *Do* you fall asleep quickly?

4 Grammar for Writing
Writing Survey Questions About Habits and Routines

Pre-writing Task

1 page 108

Answers will vary.

2 page 108

1. <u>Do</u> the <u>people</u> in your home help with the housework and chores?
2. <u>Do</u> the <u>people</u> in your home (usually) help each other when there are problems?
3. <u>Do you</u> (ever) spend time together and talk about your lives?
4. <u>Do</u> the <u>people</u> in your home enjoy each other's company?
5. <u>Does everyone</u> eat meals together?
6. <u>Do you</u> think that you have a good living situation?

Writing Task

1 Write page 109

Answers will vary.

2 Self-Edit page 109

Answers will vary.

10 Simple Present Information Questions
Cultural Holidays

1 Grammar in the Real World

A page 110

Answers will vary; Possible answer: The Day of the Dead is a time to remember dead relatives and friends.

B Comprehension Check page 111

1. b   2. a   3. c   4. a

C Notice page 111

1. When
2. Where
3. What
Do comes after *when, where,* and *what.*

2 Simple Present Information Questions

Exercise 2.1 Questions with *Who, What, When Where, How*

A page 113

2. When do
3. Who do
4. What do
5. Where do
6. How do

B Over to You pages 113–114

1. A: What celebration do you like the best?
   B: *Answers will vary.*
2. A: When do you celebrate it?
   B: *Answers will vary.*
3. A: Who do you celebrate it with?
   B: *Answers will vary.*
4. A: What do you usually do?
   B: *Answers will vary.*
5. A: Where do you celebrate it?
   B: *Answers will vary.*
6. A: What do you usually eat?
   B: *Answers will vary.*
7. A: When does it usually end?
   B: *Answers will vary.*

C Pair Work page 114

Answers will vary.

Exercise 2.2 Questions with *When* and *What Time*

A page 114

2. What time; do
3. When; does
4. What time; does
5. When; do
6. When; does
7. What time; do

B Pair Work page 114

Answers will vary.

Exercise 2.3 Asking Information Questions

A page 115

Possible answers:
2. What do people remember on this day?
3. What do towns have?
4. When does the marathon happen?
5. What time does the marathon start?
6. Where does the marathon start?
7. Who do the people watch in the marathon?

B Pair Work page 115

Answers will vary.

Exercise 2.4 Pronunciation Focus: Intonation in Questions

A page 116

2. ↗
3. ↘
4. ↘
5. ↗
6. ↗
7. ↘
8. ↗

B page 116

No answers.

Exercise 2.5 Information Questions in Titles

A page 117

2. How Does a Bird Learn to Sing?
3. Why Do People Celebrate Holidays?
4. Why Do We Grow Old?
5. What Do Teens Search for on the Internet?
6. How Do People Make New Friends?
7. Why Do We Dream?
8. When Does a Child Become an Adult?

B Over to You page 117

Answers will vary.

3 Questions with *How Often*

Exercise 3.1 Questions with *How Often*

A pages 118–119

2. How often do you drink soda?; An*swers will vary.*
3. How often do you eat breakfast alone?; *Answers will vary.*
4. How often does your family go out to a nice restaurant?;
   Answers will vary.
5. How often do your friends eat at a fast-food restaurant?;
   Answers will vary.
6. How often do your relatives visit your home?; *Answers will vary.*

B Pair Work page 119

Answers will vary.

C Over to You page 119

Answers will vary.

4 Avoid Common Mistakes

Editing Task page 120

1. How~you celebrate Thanksgiving? *(do)*
   Answer: We eat a very big meal: turkey, mashed potatoes, vegetables, and pies for dessert.
2. Where do you ~~celebrates~~ Thanksgiving? *(celebrate)*
   Answer: We usually go to my aunt and uncle's house.
3. What ~~are~~ you ~~does~~ during Thanksgiving Day? *(do do)*
   Answer: We usually go to a high school football game in the morning. Then we go to my aunt and uncle's house and watch TV.
4. What~you watch on TV? *(do)*
   Answer: Football, of course! It's a Thanksgiving tradition.
5. What time ~~are~~ you usually have your meal? *(do)*
   Answer: We usually have our meal at about 6:00 p.m.
6. What~you do on the Friday after Thanksgiving? *(do)*
   Answer: I don't go shopping! I usually sleep late and then go to the gym.
7. Why~people celebrate Thanksgiving? *(do)*
   Answer: Because it's a special day to be together with our families. We also remember the first Thanksgiving with the Pilgrims and the Native Americans.

5 Grammar for Writing
Using Questions to Write About Special Days

Pre-writing Task

1 page 121

No answers.

2 page 121

Possible answers:

Mardi Gras is a popular celebration. It takes place once *(what)*
a year for several days in February or March. Many people *(when who)*
celebrate it around the world. The celebrations are all
different. For example, in the United States, New Orleans *(what)*
is famous for its Mardi Gras celebrations. During Mardi
Gras, people wear colorful costumes and march in parades. *(what)*
Some parades are at night. Marchers throw colorful *(when)*
necklaces to the people watching the parades. The beads *(what)*
are very popular. There is a lot of jazz music and dancing. *(what)*
People love Mardi Gras because it is a good time to relax *(why)*
and enjoy life.

Writing Task

1 Write page 121

Answers will vary.

2 Self-Edit page 121

Answers will vary.

11 Conjunctions: *And, But, Or; Because*
Time Management

1 Grammar in the Real World

A page 122

Answers will vary; Possible answer: One way is to identify the important or necessary tasks for that day.

B Comprehension Check page 123

1. Most adults do not have enough time.
2. Identify the important or necessary tasks for that day. Another way is to do important tasks on the same days every week.
3. They feel good and can do more things.

C Notice page 123

1. and   3. or
2. because   4. but

2 *And, But, Or*
Exercise 2.1 Choosing *And, But, Or*

A page 124

2. , and   6. and
3. or   7. , but
4. , and   8. , but
5. , but

B Over to You page 124

Answers will vary.

Exercise 2.2 Punctuating Sentences with *And, But, Or*

A page 125

1. b. Now she listens to audiobooks in the car and during her breaks at work.
   c. She listens to a book or a podcast every day and feels good about herself.
2. a. James is very busy and often doesn't do his homework or study.

b. He worries about his grades and gets very upset.

c. Finally, he talks about his problem with a classmate, and they decide to help each other.

d. He and his classmate now talk on the phone every day and work on their homework together.

B Group Work page 125

Answers will vary.

Exercise 2.3 More *And*, *But*, *Or* page 125

Answers will vary.

Exercise 2.4 Vocabulary Focus

A page 126

2. mom
3. sisters
4. night
5. white
6. men
7. pepper
8. cash
9. jelly
10. coffee

B Pair Work page 127

Answers will vary.

3 *Because*

Exercise 3.1 Cause-and-Effect Relationships with *Because* page 128

2. e   3. b   4. a   5. f   6. g   7. d

Exercise 3.2 The Position of *Because* page 128

2. Tony can only study in the mornings *because* he thinks more clearly then.

3. *Because* Bob's alarm clock doesn't work, he is always late.

4. Jamal can't study at home *because* his roommates are too noisy!

5. *Because* Leo forgets to write his assignments down, he often misses them.

6. Tony and Jamal sometimes miss class *because* they play basketball instead.

Exercise 3.3 Combining Sentences with *Because* page 129

3. E; C; Alan has three reminders about the meeting on his phone because he doesn't want to forget about it.

4. E; C; Wanda is always hungry at work because she doesn't have time for lunch.

5. C; E; Because Karin starts work very early, she drinks a lot of coffee.

6. E; C; Because Blanca works during the day, she takes night classes.

7. E; C; Jared keeps a "to do" list because he has a lot of work.

Exercise 3.4 Giving Reasons with *Because* page 129

Answers will vary.

4 Avoid Common Mistakes

Editing Task pages 130–131

Every year, Professor Kwan teaches a class on time management. Many students like to take her class. Sometimes the class fills up quickly; because it is so popular. Students know that they need to register – early in person ~~and~~ *or* online. This is the first lesson of the time-management class.

In this class, Professor Kwan talks about different ways for students to organize their time. Her students often complain about the stress they have ~~but~~ *and* how little time they have. Professor Kwan always tells her students to buy a calendar. She says students can use an electronic calendar ~~but~~ *or* a paper calendar. ~~Because her students get organized they use their calendar every day.~~ *Her students get organized because they use their calendar every day.* She tells students to find time to study at least once a day – either after school ~~and~~ *or* at night. When students plan their time well, they feel in control and confident.

This is not the only thing that Professor Kwan teaches in the class. ~~Students~~ *Because students* have a lot of stress ~~because~~, it is also important to find time to relax; and exercise. Professor Kwan's class is so popular, because all students need help with time management. At the end of her class, students have less stress, and they have great time-management skills!

5 Grammar for Writing
Describing the Way You Do Something

Pre-writing Task

1 page 132

The writer does her homework in the library before or after her class because her homework is important.

2 page 132

I'm always busy because I work(and)I take classes. I don't have a lot of time for homework,(because)of this.(Because) my homework is important, I do it in the library before(or) after my class. The library opens at 7:00 a.m.,(and)my class starts at 8:00 a.m. The library is quiet at 7:00 a.m.(because) it is often empty then. Sometimes I ask the librarians for help. They are usually very nice(and)helpful,(but)sometimes they are busy with their work. After class, the library is full, (but)it is still a good place to study.

Connect words: and, or
Connect phrases: because
Connect clauses: and, but, because

Writing Task

1 Write page 133

Answers will vary.

2 Self-Edit page 133

Answers will vary.

12 Simple Past Statements
Success Stories

1 Grammar in the Real World

A page 134

Answers will vary.

B Comprehension Check page 135

1. False; The executive traveled to ~~London~~ *Liverpool* in December 1961
2. True
3. False; The band went to London and played on New Year's ~~Eve~~ *Day*.
4. True
5. True

C Notice page 135

1.

Present	travel	invite	play	wait	sign
Simple Past	traveled	invited	played	waited	signed

2. They end in -ed.
3.

Base Form	go	think	have	tell	become
Simple Past	went	thought	had	told	became

4. They don't end in -*ed*; their spellings are irregular.

2 Simple Past Statements: Regular Verbs

Exercise 2.1 Affirmative Simple Past Statements: Regular Verbs page 137

2. landed
3. opened
4. appeared
5. cheered; shouted
6. screamed; cried
7. played
8. watched
9. shocked
10. changed

Exercise 2.2 Negative Simple Past Statements: Regular Verbs

A page 138

2. did not learn
3. did not like
4. did not pass
5. did not believe
6. did not stop
7. did not recognize
8. did not listen

B page 138

2. showed
3. enjoyed
4. studied
5. entered
6. graduated
7. worked
8. explained
Albert Einstein

Exercise 2.3 Pronunciation Focus: Saying Simple Past Verbs

A page 139

No answers.

B Pair Work page 139

	Yes	No
3. We **talk**ed about music.		✓
4. She **want**ed to get an old album from the 1960s for her grandfather.	✓	
5. We **surf**ed the Internet.		✓
6. We **look**ed for the album.		✓
7. I **download**ed the music files.	✓	
8. We **play**ed them.		✓
9. They **sound**ed funny.	✓	
10. We **forward**ed the music files to her grandfather.	✓	
11. He **listen**ed to the songs.		✓
12. Then he **delete**d them. Not all music from the 1960s is good.	✓	

C Over to You page 139

Answers will vary.

Exercise 2.4 Vocabulary Focus: Time Expressions page 140

2. ago 4. on 6. in 8. last

3. in 5. After 7. in

Exercise 2.5 Time Expressions

Pair Work page 141

Answers will vary.

Exercise 2.6 *Did Not* and *Didn't* in Writing page 141

2. Even her family did not know about the 1,800 poems in her room.
3. In the nineteenth century, some critics did not like her work, but she continued to write for herself.
4. She did not write like other poets.
5. She did not use correct punctuation.
6. In the 1950s, poetry experts published her work again. This time, they did not edit it.

3 Simple Past Statements: Irregular Verbs

Exercise 3.1 Simple Past Statements with Irregular Verbs

A page 143

Possible answers:

2. didn't / did not read *OR* read
3. didn't / did not get up *OR* got up
4. didn't / did not come *OR* came

5. didn't / did not go *OR* went
6. didn't / did not make *OR* made
7. didn't / did not see *OR* saw
8. didn't / did not read *OR* read
9. didn't / did not have *OR* had
10. didn't / did not see *OR* saw

B Pair Work page 143

Answers will vary.

Exercise 3.2 Pronunciation Focus: Saying Irregular Simple Past Verbs

A page 143

No answers.

B page 143

Answers will vary.

Exercise 3.3 More Irregular Simple Past Verbs

A page 144

1. came; didn't / did not get; saw; Marilyn Monroe
2. made; bought; paid; Vincent van Goh
3. didn't / did not have; went; read; lost; became; Abraham Lincoln
4. wrote; told; said; bought; became; J. K. Rowling

B Group Work page 144

Answers will vary.

4 Avoid Common Mistakes

Editing Task page 145

Thomas Edison was born in 1847 in Milan, Ohio. He *did not have* ~~had not~~ very much education in school. His mother taught him reading, writing, and math. Like many children at that time, he *dropped* ~~droped~~ out of school and got a job. At age 13, he *sold* ~~sells~~ newspapers and candy at a railroad station. Thomas *continued* ~~continue~~ to learn about science by reading. At age 16, he *became* ~~become~~ a telegraph operator. Later he *started* ~~start~~ to invent things. In 1869, he moved to New York City. One of his inventions earned him $40,000, so he opened his first research laboratory in New Jersey. He tried hundreds of times to make the first lightbulb, but he *did not have* ~~had not~~ succeed. However, Thomas Edison *did not* ~~didnot~~ give up. He *learned* ~~learn~~ from his mistakes. In 1879, he *introduced* ~~introduce~~ his greatest invention, the electric light for the home. He told a reporter, "I didn't ~~failed~~ *fail* 1,000 times. The lightbulb was an invention with 1,000 steps."

5 Grammar for Writing
Writing About People in the Past

Pre-writing Task

1 page 146

Possible answer:
Tam found a job at a local grocery store. Because he was hard working, Tam became the manager of the store. In 2002, he bought the store.

2 page 146

In 1996, Tam left Vietnam and came to the United States. Life was difficult in the beginning because he didn't speak English. He took English classes at night and looked for jobs during the day. He did not find a job at first, but after several months, he found a good job at a local grocery store. Tam was very hardworking, and he learned the business very quickly. After a few years, the store owners gave Tam the job of manager. In 2002, the owners retired. Tam bought the store. The store is a very popular place in our neighborhood. Tam's story is a good success story.

Writing Task

1 Write page 147

Answers will vary.

2 Self-Edit page 147

Answers will vary.

13 Simple Past Questions
Business Ideas

1 Grammar in the Real World

A page 148

Possible answer:
For every pair of shoes he sells, he donates a pair to a child in need.

B Comprehension Check page 149

1. No
2. In 2006.
3. 1 million.
4. A lot of children have diseases because they walk barefoot. Also, the schools do not allow children without shoes.

C Notice page 149

1. finish
2. do
3. say
4. decide
Form used: base form

2 Simple Past *Yes / No* Questions

Exercise 2.1 Simple Past *Yes / No* Questions
pages 150–151

2. Did you go out
3. did you go
4. Did I tell
5. Did you see
6. Did you speak
7. Did he have

Exercise 2.2 Simple Past *Yes / No* Questions and Answers

A page 151

2. Did he have other businesses before TOMS?
3. Did his sister start the business with him?
4. Did he have any experience in fashion?
5. Did the company have difficulties at the beginning?

B page 152

2. a. Yes, he did.
   b. Yes, he started five other businesses before TOMS shoes.
3. a. No, she didn't.
   b. No, he started the business by himself.
4. a. No, he didn't.
   b. No, he didn't have any experience in fashion.
5. a. Yes, it did.
   b. Yes, it had a lot of problems.

C Pair Work page 152

Answers will vary.

Exercise 2.3 More Simple Past *Yes / No* Questions and Answers

A Over to You page 152

Answers will vary.

B Pair Work page 152

Answers will vary.

3 Simple Past Information Questions

Exercise 3.1 Simple Past Information Questions and Answers

A page 154

2. What did she do after college?
3. Who did she develop the concept with?
4. When did she open her first store?
5. What flavors did the store have?

B page 155

Possible answers:
2. She started several businesses.
3. Young Lee, her business partner.
4. In 2006.
5. Original and green tea.

4 Avoid Common Mistakes

Editing Task page 155

1. Did you ~~worked~~ *work* for a relative?
2. Who *did* you ~~worked~~ *work* for?
3. What did you ~~do~~ *do*?
4. How many hours did you ~~worked~~ *work* each week?
5. How much money did you ~~earned~~ *earn* each week?
6. ~~You enjoyed~~ *Did you enjoy* your job?
7. What *did* you ~~learned~~ *learn* from this job?
8. Why did you ~~stopped~~ *stop* working?

5 Grammar for Writing

Writing Questions About People's Activities in the Past

Pre-writing Task

1 page 156

The student admires Aunt Liz because she cares about people a lot and always helps people.

2 page 157

1. A: (What) did you do?
   B: I took care of my parents – your grandparents – when they were sick
2. A: (Why) did you do this?
   B: I helped them because they needed help. They were too sick to cook or even go to their doctors' appointments.
3. A: (When) did you do this?
   B: This happened last year when they had the flu.

4. A: (How) did you do this?
   B: I went to their house every day and did what they needed.
5. A: (Did) you work at the same time?
   B: Yes. I went to their house after my own work.
6. A: (Did) you ever complain?
   B: No, I didn't. Why should I complain? I am healthy and they're my parents.

Writing Task

1 Write page 157

Answers will vary.

2 Self-Edit page 157

Answers will vary.

14 Simple Past of *Be*
Life Stories

1 Grammar in the Real World

A page 158

Answers will vary; Possible answer: He was intelligent and a good student, but he was bored and often argued with his family.

B Comprehension Check page 159

	As a Child	As an Adult
1.	☐	☑
2.	☑	☐
3.	☑	☑
4.	☑	☐

C Notice page 159

1. was   4. was
2. were   5. were
3. was   6. was

Use *was* with a singular subject.
Use *were* with a plural subject.

2 Simple Past of *Be*: Affirmative and Negative Statements

Exercise 2.1 Simple Past of *Be*: Affirmative and Negative Statements

A pages 160–161

1. Penélope Cruz
2. was
3. was
4. was
5. was

2. Oprah Winfrey

6. was
7. were
8. was
9. was
10. was
11. was

3. Taylor Swift

12. was
13. was
14. wasn't
15. wasn't
16. weren't

B page 161

2. was	5. wasn't
3. wasn't	6. wasn't
4. was	7. was

Exercise 2.2 Simple Past of *Be:* More Affirmative and Negative Statements

A Over to You page 162

Answers will vary.

B Pair Work page 162

Answers will vary.

3 Simple Past of *Be:* Questions and Answers

Exercise 3.1 Simple Past of *Be: Yes / No* Questions

A page 164

2. Was	5. Were
3. Was	6. Were
4. Were	7. Was

B page 164

2. Yes, it was.
3. No, he wasn't.
4. Yes, they were.
5. No, they weren't.
6. No, they weren't.
7. Yes, it was.

Exercise 3.2 Simple Past of *Be: Yes / No* Questions and Information Questions

A page 165

2. Where was she born?; She was born in Wisconsin.
3. What time was she born?; She was born at 12:10 in the morning.

4. What was her father's job?; He was a store owner.
5. What was her mother's job?; She was a teacher.
6. Who was in the photo?; The writer's great-grandmother and her father were in the photo.
7. What was on the porch?; There were several chairs and some flowers on the porch.
8. Why was she angry?; She was angry because she hated sitting for pictures.
9. How old was she in the photo?; She was about three years old in the photo.

B Over to You page 166

Answers will vary.

C Pair Work page 166

Answers will vary.

4 Avoid Common Mistakes

Editing Task page 167

A: When ~~were~~ *was* Yo-Yo Ma born?

B: He *was* born in 1955.

A: ~~He~~ *Was he* born in the United States?

B: No, he wasn't. He was born in France.

A: Were his parents French?

B: No, they ~~was~~ *were* not. They ~~was~~ *were* Chinese.

A: Were his parents musicians?

B: Yes, they ~~was~~ *were* talented musicians.

A: How old was he when he first played the cello?

B: He was four.

A: How old ~~were~~ *was* he when he moved to New York City?

B: He ~~were~~ *was* five.

A: How many albums does he have?

B: Currently, he has more than 75 albums.

5 Grammar for Writing

Writing About Childhood Memories

Pre-writing Task

1 page 168

The writer's mother sang in a show. It was difficult because she was nervous / scared.

2 page 168

My mother <u>was</u> always a great singer. When she <u>was</u> 12, (there was)a talent competition at her school. My mother <u>registered</u> to sing in the show. She <u>was</u> very nervous because it <u>was</u> her first concert. The room <u>was</u> very hot. (There were)no open windows, and (there were)many people in the room. My mother <u>did not want</u> to sing because she <u>was</u> scared. Her throat <u>was</u> very dry. Then she <u>saw</u> her parents. They <u>smiled</u> at her, and that <u>helped</u> her. She <u>sang</u> her song. It <u>was</u> great! My mother often talks about this memory.

Writing Task

1 Write page 169

Answers will vary.

2 Self-Edit page 169

Answers will vary.

15 Past Time Clauses with *When, Before, and After*
Luck and Loss

1 Grammar in the Real World

A page 170

Answers will vary; Possible answer: Sandra realized the contest was a scam and called her credit card company.

B Comprehension Check page 171

1. b   2. a   3. c   4. b

C Notice page 171

1. 2, 1   2. 2, 1   3. 1, 2   4. 2, 1   5. 1, 2

2 Past Time Clauses with *When, Before, and After*
Exercise 2.1 *When, Before*, or *After*?

A page 173

2. When   6. after
3. after   7. After
4. before   8. after
5. When

B Pair Work page 173

Sentences 2 and 7.

Exercise 2.2 Ordering Events

A page 174

a. 4   b. 2   c. 3   d. 5   e. 1   f. 6

B page 174

b. He wrote a note to his wife.
c. He left for work.
d. He met a co-worker on the train.
e. He read an e-mail from the bank.
f. He called his wife.

C page 175

2. When   6. After
3. before   7. When
4. Before   8. After
5. When   9. when

Exercise 2.3 Writing Main Clauses and Time Clauses

A Over to You page 176

Answers will vary.

B Over to You page 176

Answers will vary.

C Pair Work page 176

Answers will vary.

Exercise 2.4 More Main Clauses and Time Clauses

Pair Work page 176

Answers will vary.

3 Avoid Common Mistakes

Editing Task page 177

When I got home one night two months ago, I had a voicemail message. When I listened to the message, I got excited. The message said, "Congratulations. You are a winner in our contest." *Before* I made dinner, I called the number. A woman said, "We called you two weeks ago, but you didn't answer. Please hold." After I waited for an hour, I put the phone down. *When* my wife got home, I asked her, "Did you get a message about a prize drawing?" She said, "Yes, but *after* I heard it, I deleted it. It's a scam." When she said that, I didn't say anything.

I realized my mistake; when we got the phone bill

four days later. When I read the bill, I didn't believe it. That

one-hour call cost $5,000!

4 Grammar for Writing
Telling Stories

Pre-writing Task

1 page 178

Possible answer:
Many things went wrong.

2 page 178

I had a terrible morning last week. Many things went
wrong. I grabbed my coffee (before) I left to catch the bus.
(When) I got on the bus, I didn't have my bus pass. I paid the
driver with cash and sat down. (After) I put my backpack
down, I took a sip of coffee. (When) I took a sip, the bus went
over a bump in the road, and the coffee spilled on me. I ran
to the restroom to clean up (before) I went to class. Then I
ran to class because I was late. (When) I sat down, I noticed
that the room was empty. There was no class that day
because my teacher was sick.

Writing Task

1 Write page 179

Answers will vary.

2 Self-Edit page 179

Answers will vary.

16 Count and Noncount Nouns
Eating Habits

1 Grammar in the Real World

A page 180

Answers will vary; Possible answer: Fruits and vegetables are
part of a healthy diet.

B Comprehension Check page 181

1. They help prevent different diseases.
2. It helps your heart and mood.

3. Omega-3 oil.
4. Six glasses of water a day.

C Notice page 181

1. a; a; ∅
2. ∅; ∅
3. ∅
4. a

Can count: television, newspaper, challenge
Cannot count: information, food, health, fat

2 Count and Noncount Nouns
Exercise 2.1 Count and Noncount Nouns

A page 183

	Count	Noncount
apples	✓	
beans	✓	
beef		✓
bread		✓
butter		✓
cheese		✓
cookies	✓	
fish		✓
garlic		✓
ice cream		✓
meat		✓
milk		✓
potatoes	✓	
rice		✓
sandwiches	✓	
salt		✓
seafood		✓
shrimp		✓
sugar		✓
tomatoes	✓	
vegetables	✓	
water		✓

B Over to You page 184

Answers will vary.

Exercise 2.2 *A* and *An*

A page 184

2. a	7. ∅
3. ∅	8. ∅
4. ∅	9. an; a
5. ∅; ∅	10. ∅; ∅
6. a	

B Pair Work page 184

Answers will vary.

Exercise 2.3 Count and Noncount Nouns page 185

3. s; s   9. ∅
4. s; ∅   10. s; s
5. ∅; ∅   11. s
6. ∅   12. ∅
7. ∅; ∅   13. ∅
8. s

Exercise 2.4 Singular and Plural Verbs with Nouns

A page 186

2. makes   7. contains
3. give   8. is
4. is   9. keeps
5. gives   10. gives
6. makes   11. helps

B Over to You page 186

Answers will vary.

3 Units of Measure; *How Many . . . ?* and *How Much . . . ?*

Exercise 3.1 Units of Measure pages 188–189

2. a glass of *OR* a bottle of
3. a glass of
4. a bowl of *OR* a plate of
5. a plate of
6. a piece of
7. a bag of
8. a bowl of
9. a plate of *OR* a bag of

Exercise 3.2 *How Much . . . ?* and *How many . . . ?*

A page 189

2. How much $90.00
3. How many   10
4. How much   9 bottles
5. How many   6
6. How many   16
7. How much   14 bowls
8. How much   a / 1 / one pound
9. How many   15 people
10. How much   4 pieces

B Pair Work page 190

Answers will vary.

Exercise 3.3 Categories and items

A page 191

3. furniture
4. a couch
5. equipment
6. a keyboard
7. knowledge
8. information
9. traffic
10. motorcycles
11. homework
12. an exercise
13. music
14. pop
15. money
16. a check
17. weather
18. rain

B Group Work page 191

Answers will vary.

4 Avoid Common Mistakes

Editing Task page 192

1. Where can I get ~~an~~ information about the study program?

   Look on the department website for ~~these informations~~ *this information*.

   You can also find ~~an~~ important news on the website and

   lots of helpful information.

2. How ~~much~~ *many* classes can I take each semester?

   Students can take four to six classes each semester.

3. Is there modern ~~equipments~~ *equipment* at the college?

   Yes, our kitchens have brand-new equipment! The

   college also has new ~~furnitures~~ *furniture* and computers.

4. How ~~many~~ *much* homework do professors assign?

   Every class is different, but professors will always help

   you if you have a problem with your ~~homeworks~~ *homework*.

5. Does the school give ~~an~~ advice about employment and

   ~~works~~ *work*?

   Yes! Our career counselor has ~~knowledges~~ *knowledge* about local

   employers perfect for you.

5 Grammar for Writing
Writing About Meals

Pre-writing Task

1 page 193

The writer had three problems.

2 page 193

Last (week) I cooked a (meal) for my (friends). The (food) looked good, but it wasn't very tasty. First, I served vegetable soup. It looked beautiful, but it tasted like water. Then I served fish. I gave each person a piece of salmon, but my (friends) didn't eat very much of it. It was a little dry. We had mashed (potatoes), but they were a little salty. For (dessert), I gave everyone a piece of apple (pie) and vanilla ice cream. Fortunately, the (pie) and the ice cream were delicious. My (friends) were happy and we had a good time together. I decided to invite my (friends) for another (meal) soon.

Writing Task

1 Write page 193

Answers will vary.

2 Self-Edit page 193

Answers will vary.

17 Quantifiers: *Some, Any, A Lot Of, A Little, A Few, Much, Many*
Languages

1 Grammar in the Real World

A page 194

Possible answer: Some come from Hindi and Arabic.

B Comprehension Check page 195

1. Hindi.
2. Model, baby, and CD.
3. Yes.
4. English.

C Notice page 195

1. some
2. some
3. any

Some is used in affirmative statements; *any* is used in questions

2 Quantifiers: *Some* and *Any*
Exercise 2.1 Statements with *Some* and *Any*

A page 197

2. any	6. some
3. some	7. some
4. some	8. any
5. any	9. some

B Over to You page 197

Answers will vary.

Exercise 2.2 *Yes / No* Questions with *Some* and *Any*

A pages 198–199

2. Do you have any friends from there
3. Do you have any classmates from Latin America
4. Are there any students from South Asia
5. Do you want some cookies
6. Do you have any milk
7. Can I listen to some music
8. Are there any salsa clubs around here
9. Do you want to take some dance lessons

B Pair Work page 199

No answers.

Exercise 2.3 Statements and Questions

A page 199

2. own some *OR* don't / do not own any
3. have some *OR* don't / do not have any
4. know some *OR* don't / do not know any
5. know some *OR* don't / do not know any
6. watch some *OR* don't / do not watch any
7. download some *OR* don't / do not download any
8. have some *OR* don't / do not have any
9. write some *OR* don't / do not write any
10. use some *OR* don't / do not use any

B Pair Work page 199

Answers will vary.

3 Quantifiers: *A Lot Of, A Little, A Few, Much, Many*
Exercise 3.1 Count and Noncount Nouns
page 202

Count nouns: student, song, word
Noncount nouns: homework, furniture, time, music, knowledge, Korean (language)

Exercise 3.2 *A Lot Of, A Little, A Few,* or *Many*
pages 202–203

2. many	7. a little
3. a few	8. a little
4. a lot of	9. a lot of
5. a few	10. a little
6. a lot of	11. many

Exercise 3.3 *A Lot Of, A Little, A Few, Much,* or *Many*

A page 203

2. many	6. a lot
3. a few	7. a lot of
4. many	8. a lot of
5. a lot of	

B Pair Work page 203
Answers will vary.

Exercise 3.4 Short Answers page 204

2. A little / Not much.
3. Not many
4. Not much
5. A few

Exercise 3.5 *A Lot Of, Much,* and *Many*

A page 205

In the twentieth century, a̶ ̶l̶o̶t̶ ̶o̶f̶ *many* young people had pen pals from other countries. They wrote letters to them and learned about other countries, cultures, and languages. Traveling was expensive, so they did not have a̶ ̶l̶o̶t̶ ̶o̶f̶ *many* opportunities to meet their pen pals. There was not a̶ ̶l̶o̶t̶ ̶o̶f̶ *much* direct contact between people from different countries, so letters were a good way to communicate.

Now there are not a̶ ̶l̶o̶t̶ ̶o̶f̶ *many* traditional pen pals. Instead, there are a̶ ̶l̶o̶t̶ ̶o̶f̶ *many* social networking sites on the Internet. People can send electronic messages across the world from these sites. Most young people are very busy and do not have a̶ ̶l̶o̶t̶ ̶o̶f̶ *much* time to write long messages, so messages are short. Today, friends typically send a̶ ̶l̶o̶t̶ ̶o̶f̶ *many* messages, one after another. However, can people exchange a̶ ̶l̶o̶t̶ ̶o̶f̶ *much*

information in very short online messages? Can people learn a̶ ̶l̶o̶t̶ ̶o̶f̶ *many* interesting things about the other person's culture in these short messages? This is a good question for discussion.

B Pair Work page 205
Answers will vary.

4 Avoid Common Mistakes
Editing Task pages 206–207

Roberto: Hello, Dr. Sutton. My name is Roberto Ferrer and I'm a student here at the college. I'd like to ask you a̶n̶y̶ *some* questions about the Language Center for our college paper. How does the Language Center help language students?

Dr. Sutton: Thanks for asking, Roberto. The center is very important. We give students m̶u̶c̶h̶ *a lot of* information about foreign languages and cultures, and we have m̶u̶c̶h̶ *a lot of* learning material for 30 different languages.

Roberto: Wow, that sounds like m̶u̶c̶h̶ *a lot of* information on different languages that students can find here.

Dr. Sutton: It is, Roberto. M̶u̶c̶h̶ *Many* students find the center really helpful. You see, m̶u̶c̶h̶ *many* students work and do not have m̶a̶n̶y̶ *much* time to study. They can come to the center before or after class. They can spend a few minutes or one or two hours here. They can do a̶n̶y̶ *some* exercises, or use our CDs and DVDs, or read, or just meet friends.

Roberto: That sounds great. Do m̶u̶c̶h̶ *many* students use the center?

Dr. Sutton: Right now, about 100 students use the center every day.

Roberto: Does the center have modern equipment?

Dr. Sutton: Yes, it does. Every year, we buy a̶ new

equipment, for example, computers and DVD players. We also spend ~~much~~ *a lot of* money to make the center a comfortable place. For example, we recently bought ~~a~~ new furniture. Please come and visit! We are open every day.

Roberto: All right. Thanks for your time, Dr. Sutton!

5 Grammar for Writing
Writing About Indefinite Quantities of Things

Pre-writing Task

1 page 208

Arabic uses clothing, computer, and food English loanwords. The writer writes about Arabic loanwords in English *coffee* and *sofa*.

2 page 208

I am from Oman. In Oman we speak Arabic. We have (a lot of) English words in our language. Classical Arabic does <u>not</u> have <u>any</u> English loanwords, but modern Arabic has (a lot). We use <u>a few</u> clothing words. For example, we say *jeans*, *jacket*, and *T-shirt*. We also use (many) English computer words, such as *format*, *save*, and *file*. There are <u>a few</u> English words for food in our language, such as *hot dog*, *hamburger*, and *ice cream*. (A lot of) young people use the word *cool*. There are (many) Arabic words in other languages, too. <u>Some</u> Arabic words in English are *coffee* and *sofa*. Not (many) people know that these words originally came from Arabic.

Writing Task

1 Write page 209

Answers will vary.

2 Self-Edit page 209

Answers will vary.

18 Articles: *A / An* and *The*
Changes and Risks

1 Grammar in the Real World

A page 210

Answers will vary.

B Comprehension Check page 211

1. a   2. b   3. a   4. c

C Notice   page 211

	a	an
1. ostrich		✓
2. car	✓	
3. new job	✓	
4. important decision		✓
5. business	✓	

A is used with words that begin with a consonant sound. *An* is used with words that begin with a vowel sound.

2 Articles: *A / An* and *The*
Exercise 2.1 Sentences with *A / An*

A page 213

2. An   7. a
3. An   8. an
4. a   9. a
5. an   10. an; an
6. a

B Over to You page 213

Answers will vary.

Exercise 2.2 Pronunciation Focus: Pronouncing *A* and *An*

A page 214

No answers.

B page 214

2. a   9. an
3. a   10. an
4. a   11. an
5. a   12. an
6. an   13. a
7. a   14. a
8. an

C Pair Work page 214

No answers.

Exercise 2.3 *A / An* or *The*?

A page 215

2. an   10. a
3. The   11. The
4. a   12. a
5. the   13. a
6. a   14. the
7. a   15. the
8. the   16. a
9. The

B page 216

2. the
3. an
4. a
5. a
6. an
7. a

8. The
9. The
10. The
11. the
12. the
13. the / a

C Pair Work page 216

Possible answers:
Emma is a rock climber because she is taking a risk with her business. Martin is an analyst because he takes some risks, but only after balancing the choices.

3 Article or No Article?

Exercise 3.1 *The* or *No* Article?

A page 218

2. ∅
3. ∅
4. ∅
5. the
6. The

7. the
8. ∅
9. ∅
10. ∅
11. ∅

B page 218

No answers.

Exercise 3.2 More Practice with *The* and No Article

A page 219

2. the
3. ∅
4. ∅
5. ∅
6. ∅
7. the
8. the
9. the / ∅

10. ∅
11. ∅
12. ∅
13. The
14. ∅
15. ∅
16. ∅

B Over to You page 219

Answers will vary.

Exercise 3.3 *The* and No Article with Languages and Geographic Places page 220

2. the
3. the
4. the
5. the
6. ∅
7. ∅
8. ∅

9. ∅
10. ∅
11. the
12. ∅
13. ∅
14. ∅
15. the

4 Avoid Common Mistakes

Editing Task page 221

1. I read an interesting article about how ~~the~~ people manage risk.

2. The professor gave us ~~an~~ *a* lecture on economics.

3. *An* ~~A~~ ostrich worries about getting a good job when he or she finishes college.

4. Analysts hope they have ~~an~~ insurance at work but will find ~~an~~ *a* new job if they need to.

5. Some people feel ~~a~~ fear when they have to move to a new country.

6. I hope to become ~~an~~ *a* volunteer in ~~the~~ South America after ~~the~~ college.

7. I don't speak ~~the~~ Spanish, so that's ~~an~~ *a* risk. But maybe it can be fun!

5 Grammar for Writing

Writing About Risks and Challenges

Pre-writing Task

1 page 222

The writer's friend is a "rock climber." She invites new friends to dinner parties and cooks new dishes.

2 page 222

My friend Dara is ⓐ rock climber. <u>Risks</u> and <u>stress</u> excite her. <u>Life</u> is not fun for her without <u>risks</u>. She says that they help her feel alive. For example, Dara often has large dinner <u>parties</u>. She invites new <u>friends</u> to her dinner <u>parties</u>, and she always cooks new <u>dishes</u>. My dinner <u>parties</u> are always with old <u>friends</u>. I prefer to cook for <u>people</u> I know. I never cook new <u>things</u>. It's too stressful. Sometimes Dara's <u>parties</u> are fun, and sometimes they are <u>disasters</u>. <u>The</u> last dinner party was ⓐ disaster. <u>The</u> guests did not like each other, and <u>the</u> food wasn't very good, but Dara doesn't care. She already has plans for another dinner party.

Writing Task

1 Write page 223

Answers will vary.

2 Self-Edit page 223

Answers will vary.

19 Possessive Pronouns and Indefinite Pronouns

Meals Around the World

1 Grammar in the Real World

A page 224

Answers will vary.

B Comprehension Check page 225

United States	Hong Kong	Mexico
☑ cereal	☐ cereal	☐ cereal
☑ coffee	☐ coffee	☑ coffee
☐ dumplings	☑ dumplings	☐ dumplings
☐ tea	☑ tea	☐ tea
☐ French bread	☐ French bread	☑ French bread

C Notice page 225

1. b   2. b   3. a

2 Possessive Pronouns

Exercise 2.1 Possessive Pronouns page 227

2. Did you finish yours?
3. Theirs tasted delicious.
4. John didn't take mine; he took hers!
5. Oh, you can have ours.
6. His is probably the best.
7. I like fruit with mine.

Exercise 2.2 More Possessive Pronouns

A page 228

2. theirs   5. his
3. yours   6. hers
4. theirs

B Over to You page 228

Answers will vary.

Exercise 2.3 Possessive Pronouns, Possessive Determiners, and Verbs

A page 229

2. hers   9. is
3. her   10. mine
4. are   11. mine
5. hers   12. Whose
6. Her   13. ours
7. theirs   14. who's
8. yours

B Pair Work page 229

No answers.

Exercise 2.4 Vocabulary Focus: *Theirs* and *There's* page 230

2. there's
3. theirs
4. there's
5. Theirs
6. Theirs

3 Indefinite Pronouns

Exercise 3.1 Indefinite Pronouns with -*one*, -*body*, or -*thing*

A page 232

2. thing
3. thing
4. body *OR* one
5. body *OR* one
6. body *OR* one
7. thing
8. thing

B Pair Work page 232

Sentences 4, 5, and 6 have more than one answer.

Exercise 3.2 *Yes* / *No* Questions with Indefinite Pronouns

A page 233

2. anyone *OR* anybody
3. anyone *OR* anybody
4. anything
5. anyone *OR* anybody *OR* someone *OR* somebody
6. anything *OR* something

B Pair Work page 233

Answers will vary.

Exercise 3.3 Indefinite Pronouns

A page 233

2. anything
3. everything
4. someone
5. anyone
6. Someone
7. anybody
8. anyone

B Pair Work page 233

No answers.

Exercise 3.4 Indefinite Pronouns with *-one* and *-body*   page 234

	Speaking	**Writing**
someone	☐	☑
everybody	☑	☐
anybody	☑	☐
anyone	☐	☑
no one	☐	☑
everyone	☐	☑
somebody	☑	☐
nobody	☑	☐

4 Avoid Common Mistakes

Editing Task   page 235

Everyone has a favorite sandwich shop in town, and the Snack Stop is definitely mine ~~favorite~~. I eat sandwiches
a lot, and ~~there's~~ *theirs* are the best. What do you think? Please leave a comment and let me know!

Comments:

Richard: I ate there once with my brother and sister, but I didn't like it. Everyone says the sandwiches are delicious, but ours ~~sandwiches~~ weren't good at all. Plus, my sister ordered dessert, but the server didn't bring her ~~nothing~~ *anything*. We had to remind him of our order. Then he charged my brother for French fries, but the fries were ~~mines~~ *mine*.

Jeff: Wow. I remember the first time I ate at the Snack Stop. It was with my cousin. My sandwich was delicious, and so was hers ~~sandwich~~. In fact, there wasn't ~~nothing~~ *anything* wrong with the whole meal.

5 Grammar for Writing
Writing About an Event

Pre-writing Task

1   page 236

The writer's special event is his / her parents' potluck dinner. The writers' cousins, aunts, uncles, and friends come to it.

2   page 236

On the first Sunday of every month, we have a big potluck dinner party at my parents' house. At about 5:00 p.m., (everyone) starts to arrive. My cousins and my aunts and uncles always come. In addition, some of us bring friends. My parents often invite (someone) from work. (Everyone) brings something to eat. There is always a lot of excellent food. (No one) leaves our dinner parties hungry! (Everyone) always goes home full. Usually (everyone) takes something home with them for lunch the next day. Cleanup is always a big job, but (everyone) helps. I always enjoy those Sunday dinners!

The verbs are singular.

Writing Task

1 Write   page 237
Answers will vary.

2 Self-Edit   page 237
Answers will vary.

20 Imperatives
Social Customs

1 Grammar in the Real World

A   page 238
Answers will vary; Possible answer: Be friendly and look at people when you talk to them.

B Comprehension Check   page 239

	Yes	**No**
1.	☑	☐
2.	☐	☑
3.	☐	☑
4.	☐	☑
5.	☑	☐

C Notice   page 239

1. Say
2. Look
3. Don't interrupt
4. Smile
b., d.

2 Imperatives

Exercise 2.1 Imperatives: Advice

A page 241

2. Take *OR* Don't / Do not take
3. Enjoy *OR* Don't / Do not enjoy
4. Eat *OR* Don't / Do not eat
5. Socialize *OR* Don't / Do not socialize
6. Talk *OR* Don't / Do not talk
7. Talk *OR* Don't / Do not talk
8. Learn *OR* Don't / Do not learn

B Pair Work page 241

Answers will vary.

C Over to You page 241

Answers will vary.

Exercise 2.2 Imperatives: Social Customs

A page 242

2. Take
3. Wrap
4. Don't eat
5. Don't give
6. Keep
7. Wear
8. Don't forget

B Over to You page 242

Answers will vary.

Exercise 2.3 Imperatives: Signs

A page 243

2. Don't / Do not feed
3. Don't / Do not ride
4. Don't / Do not drink
5. Don't / Do not bring
6. Don't / Do not turn
7. Don't / Do not use
8. Wear

B Pair Work page 244

Answers will vary.

C Over to You page 244

Answers will vary.

Exercise 2.4 Imperatives: Directions

A page 245

Possible answer:
Go straight on 5th Avenue. Cross Coast Road. Take a right on the next road. Turn left on 4th Avenue.

B Pair Work page 245

Answers will vary.

Exercise 2.5 Imperatives with *Always* and *Never*

A page 246

2. Never
3. Always
4. Never
5. Always
6. Always

B Over to You pages 246–247

Answers will vary.

3 Avoid Common Mistakes

Editing Task page 247

    Don't
1. ~~Dont~~ be late for class.
    Don't / Do not
2. ~~No~~ stand up when the teacher walks into the classroom.
    Don't / Do not
3. ~~Donot~~ use the teacher's first name.
    Don't / Do not
4. ~~No~~ forget to write the date your assignment is due.
    Don't / Do not
5. ~~Dont~~ forget your homework assignment.
    Don't / Do not
6. ~~Do'nt~~ copy another student's homework.
    Don't / Do not
7. ~~Donot~~ buy or download essays on the Internet.
    Don't / Do not
8. ~~D'ont~~ listen to your MP3 player in class.
    Don't / Do not
9. ~~No~~ answer your cell phone in class.
    Don't / Do not
10. ~~Don't~~ sent or read text messages in class.

4 Grammar for Writing

Writing Travel Tips

Pre-writing Task

1 page 248

Answers will vary.

2 page 248

    Hawaii is a wonderful place to visit. Here are some useful travel tips.
- Before you leave your home, (pack) carefully. <u>Pack clothes that are light and don't weigh a lot. Also, pack a raincoat. It often rains in Hawaii.</u>
- (Don't go) outside without sunscreen. <u>The sun is very strong.</u>

- Learn some words in Hawaiian. *Mahalo* means "thank you." When you meet someone, (say) *Aloha.* (Say) *Aloha* again when you leave.
- When you are in the water, (don't turn away) from the ocean. Small waves can change to big waves very quickly.
- (Don't leave) Hawaii without a *lei.* A lei is a necklace of flowers. You wear it around your neck. (Hang) it over your door after you get home for good luck.

Writing Task

1 Write page 249

Answers will vary.

2 Self-Edit page 249

Answers will vary.

21 Ability and Possibility
Making Connections

1 Grammar in the Real World

A page 250

Answers will vary.

B Comprehension Check page 251

Possible answers:
1. People can make their own websites and blogs, can share pictures, and can communicate by e-mail and texting.
2. Friends can share news and pictures.
3. We can communicate on social networking websites.

C Notice page 251

1. could not
2. can
3. can
4. could

After *can* and *could,* the base form of the verb is used.

2 *Can* and *Could* for Ability and Possibility

Exercise 2.1 *Can* and *Could* for Ability and Possibility

A page 253

2.	can	8.	couldn't
3.	couldn't	9.	can
4.	can	10.	can
5.	can	11.	can
6.	couldn't	12.	can
7.	can	13.	can't

B page 254

2. Can you send an e-mail from your phone?
3. When can you check your e-mail?
4. Where can I buy a good computer?
5. How can I learn to design websites?
6. Could you send an e-mail five years ago?
7. Can your parents use e-mail?
8. Could your parents connect to the Internet five years ago?
9. Who could send text messages 10 years ago?
10. Could you send an attachment five years ago?
11. Can you text quickly?
12. How could people communicate 20 years ago?

C Pair Work page 254

Answers will vary.

Exercise 2.2 Pronunciation Focus: Saying *Can* and *Can't*

A page 255

No answers.

B page 255

	Gen 5 website	Linkage website
1.	✓	✗
2.	✓	✓
3.	✓	✓
4.	✗	✓
5.	✗	✓
6.	✓	✗

C Pair Work page 255

Answers will vary.

3 *Be Able To* and *Know How To* for Ability

Exercise 3.1 Expressing Ability with *Be Able To* and *Know How To* page 258

2. knows
3. Do
4. don't
5. are
6. am
7. do
8. know
9. is
10. isn't
11. Do
12. know
13. are

Exercise 3.2 Expressing Ability with *Be Able To* and *Know How To*

A page 259

2. doesn't / does not know how to
3. isn't / is not able to
4. is able to
5. aren't / are not able to
6. aren't / are not able to
7. don't / do not know how to
8. are able to

B page 260

2. know how to *OR* can *OR* am able to
3. can *OR* am able to
4. can
5. Are; able to
6. can't *OR* are able to
7. can *OR* 're able to
8. can

C Pair Work page 260

Answers will vary.

4 Avoid Common Mistakes

Editing Task page 261

Dear Friends and Family,

     Now we ~~cans~~ *can* use this site to stay in touch. We can ~~shares~~ *share*

pictures and also write comments. I can ~~to~~ read your

comments on my pictures and your messages.

     My schedule this semester is busy. Last semester I ~~can~~ *could*

eat lunch in the cafeteria. This semester I have class at

lunchtime. I ~~cans~~ *can* eat lunch on the bus home, but I don't. I

just eat when I get home.

     I made a new friend yesterday. His name is Jonas. He's

very smart. He can ~~writes~~ *write* English very well, so he ~~cans~~ *can* help

me with my homework.

     Remember to write to me!

I miss you,

Jenny

5 Grammar for Writing
Writing About Abilities

Pre-writing Task

1 page 262

Possible answer: Students can understand teachers and reply in English, register for classes, use computers, use different programs on the computers in the lab, write homework with Word, and e-mail homework to teachers

2 page 263

Skills	Before entering school, students . . .	After one year, students . . .
1.	could not understand much English.	can understand their teachers.
2.	didn't know how to register for classes.	know how to choose classes. can register for their classes online.
3.	were not able to use computers.	know how to use computers. know how to use different programs on the computers in the lab. can write their homework with Word. are able to e-mail their homework to their teachers.

Writing Task

1 Write page 263

Answers will vary.

2 Self-Edit page 263

Answers will vary.

22 Requests and Permission
College Life

1 Grammar in the Real World

A page 264

Answers will vary; Possible answer: An academic adviser can help with choosing the right classes, giving advice, giving information about tutors, solving problems, problems with a class, etc.

B Comprehension Check page 265

1. Yes   3. Yes
2. No   4. Yes

C Notice page 265

1. Can   3. Can
2. Could   4. Would

The purpose of these questions is to request something.

2 *Can*, *Could*, and *Would* for Requests

Exercise 2.1 Using *Can*, *Could*, and *Would* in Requests and Answers

A page 268

2. Can   6. Could
3. can   7. Would
4. Can   8. can't
5. Would

B Pair Work page 268

No answers.

Exercise 2.2 Making and Answering Requests

A page 269

2. Can / Could / Would you meet me at the cafeteria after class today?
3. Can / Could / Would you tell me the things that I need to put in the résumé?
4. Can / Could / Would you show me your résumé?
5. Can / Could / Would you advise me on the correct style for a résumé?
6. Can / Could / Would you correct my mistakes?
7. Can / Could / Would you help me arrange my résumé so it looks good?
8. Can / Could / Would you read my résumé and make sure it's OK?

B Pair Work page 269

Answers will vary.

3 *Can*, *Could*, and *May* for Permission

Exercise 3.1 Requests for Permission with *Can*, *Could*, and *May*

A page 271

2. May   5. May
3. May   6. Can
4. Could

B Pair Work page 271

Answers will vary.

Exercise 3.2 More Requests for Permission

A page 272

Answers will vary.

B Pair Work page 272

Answers will vary.

Exercise 3.3 Formal Requests for Permission page 273

2. Could I please come to your office
3. May I ask you
4. can I please send you
5. Could I please take
6. May I e-mail
7. May I please put
8. could I please visit

Exercise 3.4 Forming Requests for Permission page 274

Possible answers:

2. Can I use your pen, please? *OR* Can I please use your pen?
3. Could I change the channel, please? *OR* Could I please change the channel?
4. May I hand in my homework one day late, please? *OR* May I please hand in my homework one day late?
5. May I speak with you after work today, please? *OR* May I please speak with you after work today?
6. Can I borrow your electronic dictionary, please? *OR* Can I please borrow your electronic dictionary?
7. May I charge my cell phone in the office, please? *OR* May I please charge my cell phone in the office?
8. May I use the atlas behind the reference desk, please? *OR* May I please use the atlas behind the reference desk?
9. Can I borrow your bicycle, please? *OR* Can I please borrow your bicycle?
10. May I get your email address, please? *OR* May I please get your email address?

4 Avoid Common Mistakes

Editing Task page 275

Hi Everyone,

The show is next week!

- Everyone: ~~You can~~ *Can you* please make a list of the equipment you need?
- Gregori: ~~You can~~ *Can you* tell me how many microphones we need?
- Jason: Could we ~~to borrow~~ *borrow* your microphone, please?

Thanks!

- Anna: We need a laptop from the computer lab. Can you
  pick
  ~~to pick~~ it up today?
  Can / Could / Would
- Jessie: ~~May~~ you contact Mr. Sparks about the lights?
  Can you
- Hector: Your job is to get the chairs. ~~You can~~ please

  arrange that?
  Can / Could / Would
- Mari: Mr. Sanchez has the music CDs. ~~Do~~ you please

  contact him?
  borrow
- Hong-yin: May we ~~to borrow~~ your projector, please?
  can / could / would
  Finally, ~~may~~ you all please come to the meeting at

2:00 p.m. tomorrow in Room 305?

Thanks!

Kazuo

5 Grammar for Writing

Writing to Ask for Permission and to Make Requests

Pre-writing Task

1 page 276

c

2 page 276

Dear Professor Harper:

 <u>Could</u> I miss my grammar tutoring appointment today? I'm very sorry, but my boss called me this morning. He needs me at work this afternoon because a co-worker is sick and she can't go to work. <u>Would</u> you have time for an appointment tomorrow morning? I am at school every Wednesday from 8:00 a.m. until noon. Also, <u>may</u> I bring a paper for my writing class to our appointment, too? The paper is due on Thursday. <u>Would</u> you be able to help me with my grammar mistakes on that paper?
Sincerely,
Clara Marcos
The e-mail is formal.

Writing Task

1 Write page 277

Answers will vary.

2 Self-Edit page 277

Answers will vary.

23 Present Progressive
Body Language

1 Grammar in the Real World

A page 278

Answers will vary; Possible answer: Body language is a crucial part of face-to-face communication.

B Comprehension Check page 279

1. b   2. a   3. a

C Notice page 279

1. are listening
2. are; telling
3. are thinking
Each verb has two parts: the first part is a *be* verb and the second is a verb + *-ing*. All the verbs in the exercise describe actions/events that are in progress.

2 Present Progressive Statements

Exercise 2.1 Present Progressive Verb Forms

A page 281

2. is leaning
3. is smiling
4. is listening
5. are making
6. are getting
7. aren't getting
8. aren't smiling
9. isn't looking
10. is leaning
11. isn't talking
12. are having

B Pair Work page 281

Answers will vary.

Exercise 2.2 Statements

A page 282

2. Pedro is chewing his pen.
3. Carlos and Eun aren't / are not sitting up straight.
4. Ana and Kerry are talking.
5. Lee and Tyler aren't / are not looking each other in the eye.
6. Yumi isn't / is not smiling.
7. Maria is staring at the door.
8. The teacher is writing on the board.

B Over to You page 282

Answers will vary.

Exercise 2.3 Vocabulary Focus: Time Expressions page 283

Possible answers:

3. 'm / am waiting
4. Today OR This semester OR This year OR This morning / afternoon / evening OR This week
5. 're / are studying
6. 'm / am enjoying
7. Tonight OR Today OR This week OR This morning / afternoon / evening OR This week
8. 'm / am writing
9. 'm / am taking
10. this semester OR this year
11. 'm / am not playing
12. right now OR this semester OR this month OR this year
13. 'm / am working
14. 're / are planning
15. 'm / am saving
16. 's / is staying
17. 's / is enjoying
18. is starting

Exercise 2.4 Negative Contractions page 284

2. isn't coming
3. isn't going
4. aren't getting
5. isn't doing
6. isn't reading
7. isn't coming
8. aren't feeling
9. aren't speaking
10. isn't doing
11. aren't giving

3 Present Progressive Questions
Exercise 3.1 Yes / No Questions and Answers page 286

2. you're not
3. Are; studying
4. I am
5. are; watching
6. I'm not
7. Are; speaking
8. they are
9. is saying
10. Are; telling

Exercise 3.2 Forming Questions and Answers

A page 287

2. What are your classmates doing right now?
3. What is your teacher saying?
4. Who is listening to the teacher?

5. What is happening in class right now?
6. Are you sitting up straight?

B Pair Work page 287

Answers will vary.

4 Present Progressive and Simple Present
Exercise 4.1 Statements page 289

2. is relaxing
3. crosses
4. make
5. chews
6. are chewing
7. is sitting
8. stands

Exercise 4.2 Vocabulary Focus: Some Common Stative Verbs

A page 289

2. Are; looking
3. Does; sound
4. Does; mean
5. Do; understand
6. Are; reading
7. Do; like
8. Do; mind
9. Do; feel

B Pair Work page 289

Answers will vary.

Exercise 4.3 Present Progressive or Simple Present? page 290

2. don't / do not know
3. are filming
4. look
5. aren't / are not sitting
6. are looking
7. are making
8. are talking
9. seem
10. Do; agree
11. seems
12. talk
13. tell
14. like
15. play
16. don't / do not look
17. sit

5 Avoid Common Mistakes

Editing Task page 291

               are
Talent shows ‸ becoming a very popular form of

                                             are
entertainment these days. The contestants in the shows ‸

trying to be famous. They sing every week. Millions of

people watch these shows every week.

      People like the shows for a number of reasons. First, the

shows have good music. For example, this season they are
including
~~includeing~~ a woman who sings opera. Second, viewers can

vote for the winners every week. Third, the contestants in

the shows come from ordinary backgrounds.

Progress Report – Psychology 111
                         are studying
      In my group, we ~~study~~ one talent show this semester
                              looking
called *Have You Got It?* We are ~~look~~ at the body language of
               trying   *am*
the contestants. We are ~~try~~ to see how it changes. I ‸ looking
                          writing
at hand gestures, and I am ~~writeing~~ a paper about the hand
                        is going   *am*
gestures of the losers. The paper ~~goes~~ well. I ‸ finding some

interesting things to write about.

6 Grammar for Writing

Writing About What You See

Pre-writing Task

1 page 292

Caitlin is in the lab at school doing research for a paper on weather changes.

2 page 292

Hi Mei,

    I'm in the lab at school at the moment. There are a lot of students here. All the computers are busy. It's very noisy and crowded. Marc <u>is sitting</u> next to me. He's <u>not working</u>, though. He <u>is e-mailing</u> someone. He ⟨looks⟩ angry because he <u>is sitting</u> with his arms crossed. I ⟨wonder⟩ who he <u>is writing</u> to! Our teacher <u>is walking</u> around. Some of the students <u>are raising</u> their hands for help. There are a lot of students who need help! I don't ⟨need⟩ help. My class ⟨seems⟩ easy this semester. I ⟨understand⟩ everything. <u>I'm doing</u> research for a paper on weather changes. It's pretty interesting. The weather is very nice here right now. How's the weather there these days? <u>I'm looking</u> for more ideas for my paper. That's all from me for the moment,
Caitlin

Writing Task

1 Write page 293

Answers will vary.

2 Self-Edit page 293

Answers will vary.

24 Past Progressive and Simple Past
Inventions and Discoveries

1 Grammar in the Real World

A page 294

Answers will vary; Arthur Fry.

B Comprehension Check page 294

Possible answers:
1. He was a researcher.
2. He made glue.
3. He used it to put it on his bookmarks.
4. It made Post-its.

C Notice page 295

1. was; trying
2. was; singing
3. was; thinking
4. were; trying

The first words are the past forms of *be*. The ending of the second word is *-ing*.

2 Past Progressive

Exercise 2.1 Past Progressive Statements

A pages 296–297

2. was trying; were using
3. was experimenting; was standing
4. was making; were asking
5. was feeling; was refusing

B Pair Work page 297

Answers will vary.

Exercise 2.2 Commonly Used Verbs page 298

2. was thinking about his children.
3. was watching TV.
4. were sitting in a restaurant.
5. was trying to park her car.
6. were looking at some photos.
7. was working at his computer.
8. was talking to a friend on the phone.

Exercise 2.3 Yes / No Questions and Information Questions

A page 299

3. What was he studying?
4. Were his friends meeting him at 12:30 p.m. for lunch?
5. Where were his classmates meeting him?
6. What was he doing at 3:00 p.m.?
7. What was he doing at 7:00 p.m.?
8. Who was he talking to last night?
9. Was he working on his project at 11:00 p.m.?

B Pair Work page 299

Answers will vary.

C Pair Work page 299

Answers will vary.

3 Time Clauses with Past Progressive and Simple Past

Exercise 3.1 Past Progressive and Simple Past

A pages 302–303

2. fell
3. was looking
4. got
5. were working
6. found
7. was making
8. discovered
9. was experimenting
10. noticed
11. was creating
12. was working
13. went
14. were working
15. were using
16. happened

B page 303

Same as **A.**

C Pair Work page 303

Answers will vary.

Exercise 3.2 Past Progressive and Simple Past with *When* and *While*

A pages 303–304

2. when
3. found
4. While
5. was writing

6. received
7. When
8. read
9. learned
10. realized
11. were looking around
12. when
13. saw
14. smiled
15. waved
16. didn't / did not wave
17. while
18. were working
19. saw

B Pair Work page 304

Answers will vary.

4 Avoid Common Mistakes

Editing Task page 305

Person	Question	Answer
Juno (30 years old)	*were you* What ~~you were~~ doing when Barack Obama became president?	*am* I ⌃watching TV all day.
Elsa (71 years old)	*were* What ~~was~~ you doing when the first men landed on the moon?	*listening* I was ~~listen~~ to the radio, and I ⌃*was* talking to a friend on the phone.
Pamela (18 years old)	*were* What you doing at 2:00 p.m. on your birthday?	*was* I ~~were~~ having lunch with some friends.
Andrea (37 years old)	*were* What ~~was~~ you and your husband doing at midnight last New Year's Eve?	*were* We ⌃dancing at a party at a friend's house.
Helen (52 years old)	*were you* What ~~you were~~ doing at 4:00 p.m. last 4th of July?	*were* My family and I ~~was~~ having a picnic.

5 Grammar for Writing

Writing About a Past Event

Pre-writing Task

1 page 306

Possible answer:
Susannah and Peter were both looking for someone special on Internet dating sites while the writer was trying to introduce them.

A strange coincidence (happened) last year. My friend Leslie and I <u>were having</u> lunch <u>when</u> we (started) talking about my cousin Susannah. Susannah <u>was looking</u> for someone special on Internet dating sites because she (was) single. Leslie (told) me about her friend Peter. Peter <u>was</u> also <u>looking</u> for someone special. I (talked) to Susannah about Peter. She (was) interested. Then, a little later, Susannah <u>was looking</u> on an Internet dating site <u>when</u> she (got) a message from a man named Peter. It (was) Leslie's friend. <u>While</u> I <u>was telling</u> Leslie about my cousin, Peter <u>was looking</u> at my cousin's profile on the site. They (met) a few days later, and they (started) dating.

Events that happened at the same time: (1) Susannah was looking for someone special while Peter was looking for someone special; (2) the writer was telling Leslie about Susannah while Peter was looking at Susannah's profile.
Events that interrupted other events: (1) Leslie and the writer were having lunch when they starting talking about Susannah; (2) Susannah was looking on an Internet dating site when she got a message from Peter.

Writing Task

1 Write page 307

Answers will vary.

2 Self-Edit page 307

Answers will vary.

25 Subject and Object Pronouns; Questions About Subjects and Objects
Fast Food or Slow Food

1 Grammar in the Real World

A page 308

Answers will vary.

B Comprehension Check page 309

1. Today Americans are eating more unhealthy food.
2. Their schedules are busy.
3. He has adapted popular high-calorie dishes and made them healthier.
4. She's trying to help people think about their diets.

C Notice page 309

1. they = Americans; it = unhealthy food
2. he = chef; them = popular high-calorie dishes
3. she = chef; they = people in these towns

2 Subject and Object Pronouns
Exercise 2.1 Choosing Pronouns

A page 311

2. It
3. we; they
4. they; me
5. him; He
6. It; us

B Pair Work page 311

Answers will vary.

Exercise 2.2 Using Subject and Object Pronouns

A page 311

2. they	8. them
3. them	9. we
4. they	10. it
5. it	11. us
6. they	12. it
7. it	13. It

B Pair Work page 311

Answers will vary.

3 Questions About the Subject and the Object
Exercise 3.1 Using *Who* and *What*

A page 314

2. Who
3. What
4. Who
5. What

B page 315

Ana Maria: Hi! My name is Ana Maria. What did you eat for lunch today?
Philip: I ate a <u>garden salad</u>.
Ana Maria: Who did you eat with?
Philip: I ate with <u>my roommate</u> here, <u>Mike</u>.
Ana Maria: Hi! What did you have for lunch?
Mike: I had a <u>chicken sandwich</u> and <u>fresh tomato soup</u>.
Ana Maria: Thanks! Excuse me, can I ask you some questions? Who usually cooks your dinner?
Maya: <u>My mom</u> usually does.
Ana Maria: What is your favorite dish?
Maya: Definitely my <u>mom's orange chicken</u>. It's great.
Ana Maria: Thanks so much!

Exercise 3.2 Forming Questions About Subjects and Objects

A page 315

Possible answers:
2. What did he eat?
3. Who did Kai Lin eat with?
4. What did he drink?
5. Who had a baked potato?
6. What did Kai Lin have?
7. Who had a healthier lunch?
8. Who spent less money?

B Pair Work page 315

Answers will vary.

C Group Work page 316

Answers will vary.

4 Avoid Common Mistakes

Editing Task page 317

Who eats fast food? So many of ~~we~~ *us* do.

My sister and ~~me~~ *I* started this blog because a lot of

our friends and family members had unhealthy diets.

We wanted to help ~~they~~ *them* make healthier choices. We also

wanted to give other people information to help ~~they~~ *them* make

better choices about their diet.

Alison had the idea to start a blog. ~~He~~ *She* told me about her

idea, and I liked it. Then my friend James helped Alison and

~~I~~ *me* design the site. Thanks, James!

If you have questions about fast food or about healthy

eating, just post your question or e-mail it to ~~we~~ *us*. Alison and

~~me~~ *I* read the questions every day and try to answer them.

~~He~~ *John* sent us our first question. ~~John~~ *He* wrote this: "Why do

so many Americans eat fast food?" Well, John, some people

eat it because ~~them~~ *they* have very busy schedules. Other people

eat it because it's affordable. But, of course, lots of people

just eat fast food because ~~them~~ *they* like it! We do, too! Alison

and ~~me~~ *I* just want to remind people that TOO MUCH fast

food is not a good idea!

We hope that helps.

5 Grammar for Writing

Writing About Healthy Living

Pre-writing Task

1 page 318

No answers.

2 page 319

My family tries to eat healthy foods, but this is sometimes difficult. We are often busy. Sometimes we eat in fast-food restaurants. They do not have many healthy choices on their menus, but they are changing. Now, many hamburger restaurants have salads on the menu. My sister and I try to eat them more often. We try to be careful with any extras. They can be very unhealthy, too. My mother does not like to eat burgers and fries. She never eats them when we eat at these places. But my father eats them! He eats almost anything! My brother likes to eat hamburgers. He and his friends eat them all the time.

At home, when we have time, we make traditional dishes. Most of the food is healthy. It has a lot of vegetables. Sometimes the food has some fat, but it is delicious. We try not to eat too much of it.

One problem is the desserts. My sister and I love to make them. Our mother and grandmother taught us. When we bake, we have a lot of fun. I think our mother is proud of us too. We do not have perfect habits, but we enjoy our food.

Writing Task

1 Write page 319

Answers will vary.

2 Self-Edit page 319

Answers will vary.

26 Infinitives and Gerunds
Do What You Enjoy Doing

1 Grammar in the Real World

A page 320

Answers will vary; Possible answer: She became a millionaire by the time she was 17 years old.

B Comprehension Check page 321

1. c   2. a   3. b

C Notice page 321

1. to play
2. to play
3. to advertise
4. to make
5. to develop

2 Infinitives
Exercise 2.1 Infinitives

A page 323

2. to buy
3. to reply
4. to chat
5. to spend
6. to write
7. to send
8. to miss
9. to surf
10. to watch
11. to do

B Over to You page 323

Answers will vary.

Exercise 2.2 Pronunciation Focus: Saying *To*: *Want To, Would Like To* page 324

A page 324

No answers.

B page 324

☑ careers
☐ family
☑ teaching
☑ school
☑ hobbies
☑ computers
☑ working with children
☐ friends

C page 325

2. 'd like to be
3. want to teach
4. like to work
5. want to have
6. hope to have
7. 'd like to work
8. like to spend
9. need to do
10. need to stay

D Pair Work page 325

Answers will vary.

3 Gerunds
Exercise 3.1 Gerunds

A page 327

2. learning OR reading OR writing
3. playing OR visiting
4. visiting
5. e-mailing OR visiting
6. reading
7. writing
8. doing

B Pair Work page 327

Answers will vary.

Exercise 3.2 Gerunds or Infinitives

A page 328

2. taking
3. to edit / editing
4. to work / working
5. to give
6. to use
7. to put
8. to make
9. to design
10. to sell / selling
11. adding
12. to grow / growing

B pages 328–329

2. to chat / chatting
3. to read / reading
4. checking
5. reading
6. living
7. surfing
8. to join
9. to check / checking
10. to meet / meeting
11. to give / giving
12. saying
13. to study / studying

C Pair Work page 329

Answers will vary.

Exercise 3.3 Vocabulary Focus: *Go* + Gerund

Pair Work page 330

Answers will vary.

4 Avoid Common Mistakes

Editing Task page 331

Dear Professor Carter,

    I enjoyed ~~to go~~ *going* to your class last week. I plan ~~getting~~ *to get* a job in marketing when I graduate, so I really enjoy ~~to listen~~ *listening* to your lecture. I ⌄*would* like to come to your class on Thursdays next semester because I can't attend your Monday class. I hope ⌄*to* get a job on Monday nights, but I don't ~~wanna~~ *want to* miss any classes. I ⌄*would* also like to attend your marketing and technology class next semester. May I come and talk to you about this?

Thank you,

Grace Lim

5 Grammar for Writing
Writing About Things People Like to Do

Pre-writing Task

1 page 332

The writer enjoys being with children a lot. They make the writer smile.

2 page 332

    I would like <u>to work</u> with children. I enjoy (being) with them a lot. They always make me smile. I started (babysitting) for our neighbors when I was 12. Then two years ago, I started (working) for a family. I take care of a three-year-old boy and a four-year-old girl. I like the family very much. The children are fun and well behaved. I often play music and sing with them. They love <u>to sing and dance</u>. They also enjoy (going) to the park and (seeing) friends. I would like <u>to be</u> a kindergarten teacher or a child-care worker one day. I think education is important for young children, and I think that I am a good teacher. I plan <u>to take</u> early childhood education classes at my community college.
Like without a gerund or infinitive after it is followed by *the family*.

Writing Task

1 Write page 333

Answers will vary.

2 Self-Edit page 333

Answers will vary.

27 Future with *Be Going To*, Present Progressive, and *Will*
The Years Ahead

1 Grammar in the Real World

A page 334

Answers will vary.

B Comprehension Check page 335

Possible answers:
1. One is moving to Chile to teach English, another is joining the Teach for America program, a third is starting a job as a junior designer, and the last is taking a course in publishing.
2. She wants to experience living in a different culture.
3. It places new college graduates in city schools across the country to teach for two years.
4. He used the career center.

C Notice page 335

	Now	Future
1.	☐	☑
2.	☐	☑
3.	☐	☑

2 Future with *Be Going To* or Present Progressive
Exercise 2.1 *Be Going To*

A page 338

2. are going to join
3. 'm going to look
4. 're going to do
5. 'm going to go
6. 're going to do
7. 'm going to work
8. 's / is going to be
9. 's going to take
10. are going to rent
11. 'm not going to go
12. 'm going to stay

B Pair Work page 338

Answers will vary.

Exercise 2.2 Future Use of Present Progressive

A page 339

2. 's / is arriving
3. 're / are going
4. 're / are meeting
5. are leaving
6. are; getting
7. are; staying
8. 're / are going

B Pair Work page 340

Answers will vary.

Exercise 2.3 *Be Going To* or Present Progressive

A page 340

2. is coming
3. is ordering
4. 're going to be
5. 're going to expand
6. 'm meeting
7. 're building
8. 's going to have
9. are going to start
10. isn't going to be

B Pair Work page 341

(a) the reference materials are going to come by next semester; going to expand the recycling program; the student center is going to have a food court, large bookstore, and conference rooms; the builders are going to start next week
(b) replacing the old computers; computer technician is coming on Monday; ordering new reference materials; meeting with people from the environmental studies program; building a new student center

C Group Work page 341

Answers will vary.

3 Future with *Will*

Exercise 3.1 *Will* and *Will Not* for Predictions

A page 343

2. will be
3. will make
4. will grow
5. will not use
6. will store
7. will get
8. will change
9. will not pay

B Over to You page 343

Answers will vary.

Exercise 3.2 *Be Going To* and *Will*

A page 344

2. When will that be?
3. Next week. The landlady is going to give me the key soon.
4. I'll / will help you move.
5. Great. I'll / will need all the help I can get. *OR* Great. I'm / am going to need all the help I can get.
6. Then I think I'll / will call Roberto and Ivan to help you, too.
7. That will make it much easier for me. Thanks.
8. Let's celebrate then. You're / are going to love having your own place!

B Over to You page 344

Answers will vary.

Exercise 3.3 Pronunciation Focus: Information Questions with *Will*

A page 344

No answers.

4 Avoid Common Mistakes

Editing Task page 345

Hi Nuala,

I ~~will meet~~ *am meeting* with a career adviser next week, and I *am* going to

discuss my future. What can I tell him? My dream is to work

in television or the movies. I think I *am* going to apply to a media

studies program. I ~~will~~ *am going to* take a special course or something. I

~~will~~ *am going to* talk to some people who know about careers in TV soon.

I think they *will* give me some good advice.

Can we talk about this? What ~~you are~~ *are you* doing on Monday?

I ~~will go~~ *am going* away on the weekend, but I *will* be back Monday

morning. I'll call you then.

Thanks,

Fandi

5 Grammar for Writing
Writing About Future Plans

Pre-writing Task

1 page 346

Not working full-time will give the writer time for homework at night. The writer is also going to save all his / her money in the summer.

2 page 346

I am going to finish my English classes in three semesters. I'm taking a grammar class this summer. I registered for it last week. I'm taking only one class this summer. In the fall, I'm going to take reading and conversation classes. I'm also going to take another grammar class. Three classes will be a lot of work, so I am not going to work full-time. That will give me time for my homework at night. I'm also going to save all my money this summer. That will help. There will be an online writing class in the spring. I hope to take that class. It will be my first online class. I will also need to take one more reading class. That will be my last English class!

Most certain of: finishing English classes in three semesters; taking grammar class this summer; taking three classes in the fall; not working full-time;

Result of other possibilities: having time for homework at night; saving money this summer; taking an online class

Writing Task

1 Write page 347

Answers will vary.

2 Self-Edit page 347

Answers will vary.

28 *Will, May,* and *Might* for Future Possibility; *Will* for Offers and Promises
Will We Need Teachers?

1 Grammar in the Real World

A page 348

Answers will vary.

B Comprehension Check page 349

Possible answers:
1. It's a way of attending school through the use of a computer.

2. Class materials are online, so the teacher and students can be anywhere.
3. Teachers may become "learning managers" or coaches.
4. Probably not. People will always enjoy going to class.

C Notice page 349

1. will
2. may not
3. might not
4. will

2 *May* and *Might*; Adverbs with *Will*
Exercise 2.1 *Will, May,* and *Might*

A page 351

2. 'll
3. won't
4. 'll
5. might
6. 'll
7. might
8. 'll
9. 'll

B Pair Work page 352

1. To take online courses.
2. Her family is moving, and this way she won't have to change schools.
3. Chemistry, biology, and Spanish.
4.

Sharon's Plans	
Certain	**Not Sure**
family is moving	enrolling in an online program
taking chemistry	changing schools
taking Spanish	taking biology
keeping in touch	
being online all the time	

Exercise 2.2 More *Will, May,* and *Might*

A page 352

Answers will vary.

B Pair Work page 353

Answers will vary.

C Over to You page 353

Answers will vary.

Exercise 2.3 Adverbs with *Will*

A page 354

Possible answers:

2. Teachers will probably be robots.
3. Teaches will certainly need to prepare for their classes.
4. They will likely check exercises.
5. Computer software will probably check students' work.
6. Teachers will possibly spend more time with each student.
7. They will probably not need to speak English.
8. Computer software will definitely translate from any language.

B Pair Work page 354

Answers will vary.

C Over to You page 355

Answers will vary.

D Pair Work page 355

Answers will vary.

3 Offers and Promises
Exercise 3.1 Offers and Promises

A pages 356–357

2. I'll pay you back
3. I'll show you.
4. I'll drive you home.
5. I'll make you dinner.
6. I'll look at the homework with you.
7. I'll help you with your math homework.

B Pair Work page 357

Answers will vary.

4 Avoid Common Mistakes

Editing Task pages 357–358

The Internet ~~can~~ *will* change education completely in the future. ~~May be~~ *Maybe* colleges will not be buildings with people and furniture, but complex websites. Teachers ~~maybe~~ *may be* characters in virtual worlds like *Second Life*. In the future, students ~~can~~ *will / may / might* "travel" to different countries using their computers. They ~~can~~ *will / may / might* walk around the world's famous museums without leaving home. ~~May be~~ *Maybe* students will go back in time. They ~~can~~ *may / might* possibly "talk to" famous people from the past, like George Washington. History students

~~can~~ *will / may / might* watch or be part of historic events. We ~~can~~ *will / may / might* buy artificial brains so we won't have to go to school at all! There ~~maybe~~ *may be* many changes to education, but learning ~~can~~ *will* definitely never stop.

5 Grammar for Writing
Writing About Future Predictions and Possibilities

Pre-writing Task

1 page 358

Possible answer:
Universities will be completely online in the future. This will help the pollution problem.

2 page 359

I believe that universities <u>will be</u> completely online in the future. This <u>will certainly be</u> very good for the environment. There (may not be) any physical libraries in the future because all the books (might be) in online libraries. That way, people <u>will not have</u> to cut down as many forests. Students (might meet) with their teachers on their computers. Universities <u>will surely need</u> fewer buildings and parking lots. The current university buildings (may become) apartment buildings. Students and teachers <u>will not need</u> cars and buses to get to school. This <u>will definitely help</u> the pollution problem. It (may) also (help) housing problems in some communities. I believe that online universities <u>will be</u> a very good thing.
Predictions the writer is sure of: those that include adverbs of certainty (certainly, surely, definitely).

Writing Task

1 Write page 359

Answers will vary.

2 Self-Edit page 359

Answers will vary.

29 Suggestions and Advice
Study Habits

1 Grammar in the Real World

A page 360

Possible answer:
The writer gives 14 suggestions.

B Comprehension Check page 361

1. Try listening to soft music with earphones.
2. So you can concentrate better.
3. Look at your task and decide how much you want to accomplish during the study session.
4. You should not check e-mail while you study because it's easy to get distracted.
5. Just say, "Let's meet after class and review our notes."

C Notice page 361

1. a. study; b. try; c. want
2. The base form.
3. Should.
4. Making a suggestion.

2 Suggestions and Advice

Exercise 2.1 Suggestions and Advice

A page 363

2. She should / might want to / ought to practice new words every day.
3. She should / might want to / ought to write sentences with the new words.
4. He should / might want to / ought to practice using the words with a friend.
5. They should / might want to / ought to do crossword puzzles.
6. They should / might want to / ought to create a picture in their minds that shows the meaning of each word.

B Pair Work page 363

Answers will vary.

Exercise 2.2 More Suggestions and Advice

A page 364

2. shouldn't
3. might want to
4. should probably
5. Maybe; should
6. Why don't
7. Let's
8. ought to
9. shouldn't
10. should

B Pair Work page 364

Answers will vary.

C Over to You page 364

Answers will vary.

3 Asking for and Responding to Suggestions and Advice

Exercise 3.1 Responding to Questions for Advice

A pages 366–367

Possible answers:
3. Where should
4. should probably
5. should definitely
6. Should
7. Absolutely / Definitely

B Pair Work page 367

Answers will vary.

Exercise 3.2 Asking for and Giving Advice

A page 368

Possible answers:
2. Which movie should I go to?
3. You should probably / You might want to / You ought to . . .
4. Where should I buy school supplies?
5. You should probably / You might want to / You ought to . . .
6. You shouldn't . . .
7. Why don't you . . .
8. What should I do to learn more English vocabulary?

B Pair Work page 368

Answers will vary.

C Over to You page 368

Answers will vary.

4 Avoid Common Mistakes

Editing Task page 369

Julia: Monica, I need help studying! How I should tell the professor? *(I inserted before should)*

Monica: Don't worry. I can help. First, we should shares *share* class notes.

Julia: When we should meet at the library? After class today? *(we inserted after should)*

Monica: Sure, but we ought to probably *probably* meet in the cafeteria. I'll want to eat something.

Julia: OK. We should eats *eat* dinner while we study. What I should bring? *(I inserted before should)*

Monica: Just your notebook. You ^*probably* should not ~~probably~~

bring the big textbook – I don't think we'll need it.

Julia: You should ~~to~~ be ready for a lot of questions

from me! I have so many!

Monica: As long as you are ready to learn, I'm happy to

help! When we're done, we ought ^*to* see a movie!

Julie: That sounds great! See you later!

Monica: See you then, Julie. We should ~~to~~ study together

more often!

5 Grammar for Writing
Making Suggestions and Giving Advice

Pre-writing Task

1 page 370

It's hard to study in your room because family and roommates can be very distracting. The writer suggests six study tips.

2 page 370

You may find it hard to study in your room because family and roommates can be very distracting. The library is a great place to study. Here are some suggestions for studying in the library. If possible, you <u>should</u> go to the library at the same time every day. That will help you create good study habits. When you are in the library, you <u>should not</u> sit near your friends. Instead, you <u>should</u> find a quiet place to work. You <u>ought to turn your cell phone off</u>. Every text or call is a distraction. When you are working with other students, you <u>should</u> use a study room for groups. You might want to reserve a study room in advance, especially around exam time. You cannot replace *should* with *ought to* for all sentences because *ought to* is stronger than should.

Writing Task

1 Write page 371

Answers will vary.

2 Self-Edit page 371

Answers will vary.

30 Necessity and Conclusions
Getting What You Want

1 Grammar in the Real World

A page 372

Answers will vary.

B Comprehension Check page 373

1. Yes.
2. Yes.
3. Six months before they are due.
4. Your adviser.
5. A deadline.

C Notice page 373

1. necessary   3. necessary
2. not necessary   4. necessary

2 Necessity and Conclusions with *Have To, Need To, Must*
Exercise 2.1 Necessity and Obligations

A page 376

2. has to
3. needs to
4. needs to
5. don't / do not have to
6. have to
7. have to
8. don't / do not need to
9. have to
10. must not

B page 377

2. How old does a driver have to be?
3. What do drivers have to bring to the DMV?
4. What does an acceptable document need to say?
5. Do drivers have to be citizens?
6. Do new drivers need to take a class?
7. Do new drivers have to pass an exam?
8. Where do drivers need to go to get their license?

C Pair Work page 377

Possible answers:
1. Yes.
2. 16 to 18 years old.
3. Documents proving the driver's identity.
4. Your name and address.
5. No.
6. No.
7. In some states.
8. At their local DMV.

Exercise 2.2 Pronunciation Focus: *Have To* and *Has To*

A page 377

No answers.

B page 378

2. has to
3. have to
4. have to
5. has to
6. have to
7. have to
8. have to

C Pair Work page 378

Answers will vary.

Exercise 2.3 Necessity and Conclusions

A page 379

2. must / has to be; C
3. needs to take / has to take; N
4. has to / needs to / must talk; N
5. needs to / has to / must look; N
6. has to / needs to / must make; N
7. must not do; N
8. must like; C

B Pair Work page 380

Answers will vary.

3 Avoid Common Mistakes

Editing Task page 381

Pete:	Does Jack ~~needs~~ *need* to have a lot of skill to play the game?
Jim:	No, he has to ~~has~~ *have* a lot of luck.
Pete:	How many times does he ~~has~~ *have* to win to break the record?
Jim:	He ~~have~~ *has* to win three more times.
Pete:	He won eight times, so the record must ~~to~~ be 10.
Jim:	Yes, the world record ~~needs to~~ *must / has to* be 10.
Pete:	Does he need to ~~has~~ *have* a certain time to win?
Jim:	No, he must ~~to~~ have a certain number of points.
Pete:	Jack also has to ~~wins~~ *win* five games in a row. He must ~~to~~ really like this computer game!
Jim:	Yeah, he loves it. He doesn't ~~needs~~ *have* to play it every day, but he enjoys it.

4 Grammar for Writing

Writing About Necessity and Obligation

Pre-writing Task

1 page 382

The writer writes about four people.

2 page 382

Everyone (needs to find) a way to relax or manage stress. This is particularly important before going to bed. Different people have different ways of relaxing. My aunt Flora (needs to do) something with her hands. She often knits while watching TV. My brother has a very stressful job. He has to do something to help him forget about his stressful day. He says that he <u>has to play cards or read</u> a magazine after dinner. My uncle Ralph has a lot of problems sleeping. He usually goes for a bike ride or a walk after dinner. He does not (need to be) out for a long time, but he <u>has to exercise</u> and get some fresh air. I <u>must take</u> a hot shower in the evening. Without a shower, I cannot fall asleep. And I <u>must not go</u> to bed too late, or I'll get sick. I really must try hard to get to sleep early.

The writer uses *must* to indicate a very strong obligation.

Writing Task

1 Write page 383

Answers will vary.

2 Self-Edit page 383

Answers will vary.

31 Adjectives and Adverbs
Making a Good Impression

1 Grammar in the Real World

A page 384

Answers will vary.

B Comprehension Check page 385

1. Yes; Careful preparation.
2. Yes; List three or four main points on note cards.
3. Yes; Practice by yourself and with friends. Tell your friends to give you honest feedback.
4. Yes; Ask people for feedback and advice so you will learn to give good presentations and enjoy them.

C Notice page 385

1. a. A **confident** (presenter) always makes a good impression.
   b. Think **positive** (thoughts).

2. a. (Smile) **confidently**.

    b. Before you start, (breathe) **deeply**.

The circled words in item 1 are nouns; the circled words in item 2 are verbs.

3. b

The word has to describe the verb *walks*.

2 Adjectives and Adverbs of Manner

Exercise 2.1 Adjectives and Adverbs

A page 387

I'm a (professional) hairstylist, and I'm very (good) at my job. I'm (friendly) and (polite) to my clients, so I make a (good) impression. But I don't schedule clients early in the day because I'm not in a (good) mood until noon.

Of course, I don't get an (early) start to my day. I wake up late and start my day slowly. I can't think clearly without (three) cups of (strong) coffee. After breakfast, I take a shower, get dressed, and check my e-mail. I don't talk to anyone in the morning, except for my (elderly) neighbor when I leave home. He likes to sit on the (front) porch. I think he's (lonely).

I drive to work, but my commute isn't (bad). When I get to work, I check my schedule closely and make a (few quick) phone calls. At 11:55 a.m., I finish my (last) cup of coffee and smile warmly at my (first) client at 12:00 noon.

B Over to You page 387

Answers will vary.

Exercise 2.2 More Adjectives and Adverbs

A page 388

1. b. clearly
   c. automatically
   d. strong
2. b. early
   c. careful
   d. well
   e. bad

B Pair Work page 388

Answers will vary.

Exercise 2.3 Adverbs of Manner

A page 389

2. seriously
3. hard
4. carefully
5. properly; quickly
6. appropriately
7. politely
8. well
9. neatly
10. clearly
11. closely

B Pair Work page 389

Answers will vary.

C page 389

Answers will vary.

3 Adjectives with Linking Verbs; Adjectives and Adverbs with *Very* and *Too*

Exercise 3.1 Adjectives with Linking Verbs

A page 391

2. confident; *Answers will vary.*
3. excited; *Answers will vary.*
4. uncomfortable; *Answers will vary.*
5. attractive; *Answers will vary.*
6. friendly; *Answers will vary.*
7. well; *Answers will vary.*
8. excited; *Answers will vary.*
9. easily; *Answers will vary.*
10. strongly; *Answers will vary.*

B Pair Work page 392

Answers will vary.

Exercise 3.2 Adjectives with *Very* and *Too*

A page 392

2. too
3. too
4. too
5. too
6. very
7. very
8. too
9. too
10. very

B page 392

Same as **A.**

Exercise 3.3 Adjectives with *Too* + Adjective + Infinitive

A Pair Work page 393

2. too early to say
3. too young to get married
4. not too late to change programs
5. too cold to go camping
6. too sick to go to work
7. too scared to ask
8. too busy to think

B Group Work page 394

Answers will vary.

Exercise 3.4 *Not very . . .* page 394

3. He didn't / did not wear a clean shirt.
4. He wasn't / was not very good at problem solving.
5. He didn't / did not answer questions very well.
6. He didn't / did not look very honest
7. He didn't / did not seem very experienced.
8. He didn't / did not act very interested.

4 Avoid Common Mistakes

Editing Task page 395

An interview can be a difficult experience. Prepare
~~carefully~~ *carefully* your responses and you will make a good

impression.

Before the interview, research ~~thoroughly~~ *thoroughly* the company.

Find out about its products and services. You should always

be ~~truthfully~~ *truthful* about the things you do ~~good~~ *well*. When you talk

about something you do ~~bad~~ *poorly*, choose a weakness that is

not serious. Say that you are ~~too~~ *very* aware of the weakness

and that you are working ~~hardly~~ *hard* to improve yourself. Say

you want a new challenge and that you want to progress

in your career. Always sound ~~positively~~ *positive* and don't complain

about your current job.

On the day of the interview, dress ~~nice~~ *nicely*. Shake ~~firmly~~ *firmly*

hands when you meet the interviewer. Try to sound

~~sincerely~~ *sincere* and look ~~too~~ *very* confident. Follow these steps and

you'll do ~~good~~ *well*.

5 Grammar for Writing

Writing About People's Behavior in Different Situations

Pre-writing Task

1 page 396

Possible answers:
The writer is giving tips about meeting people at parties;
Answers will vary.

2 page 396

Do you get nervous meeting new people at parties?
Many people are not very comfortable in these situations.
Some people are afraid that they are not very interesting
Other people talk too much or too loudly. Here are
some tips for making a good impression at parties. Don't
worry about finding intelligent things to say. Listen closely
to others instead. Many people can talk very happily about
themselves for a long time. Listen carefully and then ask
questions. Also, when you listen to people, make eye
contact with them. People will think you are very nice and
they will want to be your friend. These tips will help you
enjoy parties and make new friends very easily.

Writing Task

1 Write page 397

Answers will vary.

2 Self-Edit page 397

Answers will vary.

32 Comparative Adjectives and Adverbs
Progress

1 Grammar in the Real World

A page 398

Answers will vary; Possible answer: It discusses how many things have changed in terms of size, speed, and quality in the twentieth century.

B Comprehension Check page 399

1. wider; faster
2. more powerful; more complicated; easier
3. faster; smaller

C Notice page 399

1. smaller
2. bigger
3. larger
4. more efficient
5. more powerful
6. more congested

Add -er to the end of the adjective or add more before the adjective.

2 Comparative Adjectives

Exercise 2.1 Comparisons with *Be*

A page 402

2. lighter
3. quieter
4. easier
5. faster
6. safer
7. smaller
8. bigger

B page 402

Possible answers:

2. Old cell phones were bigger.
3. Old cell phones were slower.
4. Old cell phones were more expensive.
5. New cell phones are cheaper.
6. New cell phones are more powerful.
7. New cell phones are faster.
8. New cell phones are thinner.

Exercise 2.2 Comparative Adjectives and Nouns

A page 403

Possible answers:

2. a newer and safer bridge
3. cheaper parking
4. cleaner parks
5. more energy-efficient busses
6. clearer street signs
7. more frequent bus service
8. a more attractive website

B Pair Work page 403

Answers will vary.

C Group Work page 404

Answers will vary.

3 Comparative Adverbs

Exercise 3.1 Making Comparisons with Adverbs page 406

2. harder
3. later
4. further
5. less often
6. more slowly

Exercise 3.2 More Making Comparisons with Adverbs

A page 407

Possible answers:

Adverb, Comparative Adverb		Verb(s)
1. fast	faster	run, drive
2. well	better	play football / tennis; play the guitar, sing, speak English, study, drive
3. carefully	more carefully	drive, spend money, walk / run
4. hard	harder	play football / tennis; study; work
5. slowly	more slowly	drive, sing, speak English, walk / run
6. early	earlier	get up, go to bed, go to the gym, walk / run, work, go to the movies, go out, study
7. far	farther	walk / run, drive
8. frequently	more frequently	go out, go to the gym, go to the movies, play football / tennis, play the guitar, study, walk / run, drive, speak English, work, sleep, spend money, sing
9. badly	worse	drive, play football / tennis, sing, speak English, study, play the guitar
10. late	later	go out, go to bed, go to the gym, sleep, study, work, go to the movies, get up

B Over to You page 407

Answers will vary.

Exercise 3.3 Adverbs and Personal Pronouns

A Over to You page 408

3. *Answers will vary;* do.
4. *Answers will vary;* do.
5. *Answers will vary;* do.
6. *Answers will vary;* did.
7. *Answers will vary;* can.
8. *Answers will vary;* did.

B Pair Work page 408

Answers will vary.

4 Avoid Common Mistakes

Editing Task page 409

It is not easy to answer this question. Here is a list of ideas.

Lisa: Medicines are now more effective and ~~more~~ *cheaper*

~~cheap~~, so people's health is ~~more~~ better. People

expect to live longer ~~then~~ *than* they did 100 years ago.

Dan: There's a ~~more~~ shorter work week for everyone.

There are ~~powerfuler~~ *more powerful* machines and computers,

so people can be free from manual work.

Sanjay: Children reach a ~~more~~ higher level of

education.

Cristina: People have ~~more big~~ *bigger* houses and a

~~comfortabler~~ *more comfortable* life ~~that~~ *than* their parents.

5 Grammar for Writing

Making Comparisons

Pre-writing Task

1 page 410

The writer is comparing cars today from cars in the 1990s.

2 page 410

Cars are very different today from cars in the 1990s. A lot of today's cars are <u>smaller</u>. Cars today also run more efficiently. They use <u>less</u> gas, so they can go <u>further</u> on one tank of gas. Some cars are <u>easier</u> to park because they have special parking instruments, and some even park themselves! New cars have GPS systems that tell you where you are. Cars are also <u>safer</u> today. Air bags, seat belts, and <u>better</u> brakes that help you stop more quickly make them <u>safer</u>.

I think that one thing that is not <u>better</u> today is the driver. Some drivers drive less carefully these days. The main reason is that people use cell phones. Many drivers still talk on their cell phones while they drive. In many states this is illegal, but people still do it. Cars may be <u>safer</u> today, but the driver must drive safely.

Writing Task

1 Write page 411

Answers will vary.

2 Self-Edit page 411

Answers will vary.

33 Superlative Adjectives and Adverbs
Facts and Opinions

1 Grammar in the Real World

A page 412

Answers will vary.

B Comprehension Check page 413

Possible answers:
1. It is located in Southeast Asia.
2. The climate is hot and humid.
3. Hue was the home of the Nguyen Kings.
4. Crude oil is the most important export.

C Notice page 413

1. biggest
2. hottest
3. wettest
4. narrowest
5. most popular
6. most historic
7. most important
8. most beautiful

2 Superlative Adjectives
Exercise 2.1 Superlative Adjectives

A Pair Work page 416

2. largest; Asia
3. most; Africa
4. deepest; Pacific
5. biggest; Russia
6. coldest; Antarctica
7. highest; Mount Everest
8. driest; the Atacama Desert, Chile
9. largest; New York City
10. longest; the Nile
11. most populated; China

B page 417

2. the longest; the Mississippi
3. the driest; Nevada
4. the wettest; Hawaii
5. the most popular; Great Smoky Mountains National Park in Tennessee and North Carolina
6. the biggest; New York
7. the least wasteful; San Francisco
8. the most expensive; New York
9. the worst; Los Angeles
10. the most famous; the Golden Gate Bridge, California
11. the busiest; Atlanta's Hartsfield-Jackson
12. the most populated; California
13. the least populated; Wyoming

C Over to You page 417

2. most delicious; *Answers will vary.*
3. most crowded; *Answers will vary.*
4. worst; *Answers will vary.*
5. most dangerous; *Answers will vary.*
6. most unusual; *Answers will vary.*

Exercise 2.2 Superlative Adjectives to Describe People

A page 418

2. best
3. closest
4. the youngest
5. oldest
6. best
7. the most unusual
8. the most interesting
9. the most exciting
10. the most exotic
11. the highest
12. the most intelligent
13. the most successful

B page 418

Same as **A**.

C Over to You page 418

Answers will vary.

3 Superlative Adverbs

Exercise 3.1 Superlative Adverbs

A page 421

2. the longest
3. the most economically
4. the most frequently
5. the hardest
6. the latest

7. the earliest
8. the farthest

B Pair Work page 422

Answers will vary.

4 Avoid Common Mistakes

Editing Task page 423

One of the ~~more~~ *most* amazing things ~~of~~ *in* the natural world is the great variety of animal sizes and behaviors. At 200 tons (180 metric tons) and 108 feet (33 meters), the blue whale is the world's ~~heavyest~~ *heaviest* and ~~bigest~~ *biggest* animal. However, the world's ~~smaller~~ *smallest* bird weighs less than one ounce (1.8 grams). Giraffes can be 17 feet (5.2 meters) tall, and they are the tallest animals ~~of~~ *in* the world. The cheetah runs the ~~faster~~ *fastest* of all animals. It can run up to 75 miles per hour (120 kilometers per hour).

On the other hand, a sloth is perhaps the world's ~~most~~ slowest animal. It often does not move for hours. The loudest land animal is the howler monkey. You can hear its cry about 10 miles (16 kilometers) away. What is the ~~louder~~ *loudest* marine animal? The blue whale. Blue whales can hear each other up to 1,000 miles (1,600 kilometers) away. What is the animal that lived the ~~most long~~ *longest*? It is a clam from the coast of Iceland. Scientists estimate that it is 405 years old. The gastrotrich, a tiny water animal, has the ~~most short~~ *shortest* life – three days.

5 Grammar for Writing

Writing About the Most, Least, Best, and Worst of Things

Pre-writing Task

1 page 424

Four people live in the writer's house.; *Answers will vary.*

2 page 424

My roommates and I are all very good friends, but we are all very different. My roommate Sandy is the *a*

(most athletic) of us all. She is always outside playing tennis

a

or soccer. We all do those things, but Sandy is the (best) at

b

them. Shogo is the apartment's (most serious) person. He

a   *a*

works the hardest and does the best. He's going to graduate

a   *a*

the earliest. Jess is the (most social) of all of us. He is always

a

planning fun things to do. He makes friends the easiest and

a

brings home new people the most often. Our apartment's

c   *c*

(most organized) and (cleanest) person of all the roommates

a

is me! I take care of our apartment the most. It may not

sound very interesting, but someone has to do it, and I do

not mind.

The most common pattern is a.

Writing Task

1 Write   page 425

Answers will vary.

2 Self-Edit   page 425

Answers will vary.

Unit Tests with Answer Key

A ready-made Unit Test for each of the 33 units of the Student's Book is provided. The tests are easily scored, using a system found at the beginning of the Answer Key. Each test is available in both pdf and Microsoft Word formats.

Instructional PowerPoint® Presentations

The PowerPoint® presentations offer unit-specific grammar lessons for classroom use. The presentations include interactive versions of the key *Grammar Presentations* for each unit.

CD-ROM Terms and Conditions of Use

This is a legal agreement between you ("the customer") and Cambridge University Press ("the publisher") for the *Grammar and Beyond 1 Teacher Support Resource CD-ROM*.

1. **Limited license**
   (a) You are purchasing only the right to use the CD-ROM and are acquiring no rights, express or implied, to the software itself, or the enclosed copy, other than those rights granted in this limited license for educational use only.
   (b) The publisher grants you the license to use one copy of this CD-ROM on your site and to install and use the software on this CD-ROM on a single computer. You may not install the software on this CD-ROM on a single secure network server for access from one site.
   (c) You shall not: (i) copy or authorize copying of the CD-ROM, (ii) translate the CD-ROM, (iii) reverse-engineer, alter, adapt, disassemble, or decompile the CD-ROM, (iv) transfer, sell, lease, lend, profit from, assign, or otherwise convey all or any portion of the CD-ROM, or (v) operate the CD-ROM from a mainframe system.

2. **Copyright**
   All titles and material contained within the CD-ROM are protected by copyright and all other applicable intellectual property laws, and international treaties. Therefore, you may not copy the CD-ROM. You may not alter, remove, or destroy any copyright notice or other material placed on or with this CD-ROM.

3. **Liability**
   The CD-ROM is supplied "as-is" with no express guarantee as to its suitability. To the extent permitted by applicable law, the publisher is not liable for costs of procurement of substitute products, damages, or losses of any kind whatsoever resulting from the use of this product, or errors or faults in the CD-ROM, and in every case the publisher's liability shall be limited to the suggested list price or the amount actually paid by the customer for the product, whichever is lower.

4. **Termination**
   Without prejudice to any other rights, the publisher may terminate this license if you fail to comply with the terms and conditions of the license. In such event, you must destroy all copies of the CD-ROM.

5. **Governing law**
   This agreement is governed by the laws of England, without regard to its conflict of laws provision, and each party irrevocably submits to the exclusive jurisdiction of the courts of England. The parties disclaim the application of the United Nations Convention on the International Sale of Goods.